IMPOSTER
NO MORE

IMPOSTER NO MORE

OVERCOME SELF-DOUBT AND IMPOSTERISM TO CULTIVATE A SUCCESSFUL CAREER

JILL STODDARD, PHD

balance

NEW YORK BOSTON

Copyright © 2023 by Jill Stoddard

Cover design by Jim Datz. Cover photograph © Getty Images.
Cover copyright © 2023 by Hachette Book Group, Inc.

Hachette Book Group supports the right to free expression and the value of copyright. The purpose of copyright is to encourage writers and artists to produce the creative works that enrich our culture.

The scanning, uploading, and distribution of this book without permission is a theft of the author's intellectual property. If you would like permission to use material from the book (other than for review purposes), please contact permissions@hbgusa.com. Thank you for your support of the author's rights.

Balance
Hachette Book Group
1290 Avenue of the Americas
New York, NY 10104
GCP-Balance.com
Twitter.com/GCPBalance
Instagram.com/GCPBalance

First Edition: September 2023

Balance is an imprint of Grand Central Publishing. The Balance name and logo are trademarks of Hachette Book Group, Inc.

The publisher is not responsible for websites (or their content) that are not owned by the publisher.

The Hachette Speakers Bureau provides a wide range of authors for speaking events. To find out more, go to hachettespeakersbureau.com or email HachetteSpeakers@hbgusa.com.

Balance books may be purchased in bulk for business, educational, or promotional use. For information, please contact your local bookseller or the Hachette Book Group Special Markets Department at special.markets@hbgusa.com.

Library of Congress Cataloging-in-Publication Data
Names: Stoddard, Jill A., author.
Title: Imposter no more : overcome self-doubt and imposterism to cultivate a successful career / Jill Stoddard, PhD.
Description: First edition. | New York : Balance, [2023] | Includes bibliographical references and index.
Identifiers: LCCN 2023016030 | ISBN 9781538724798 (hardcover) | ISBN 9781538724811 (ebook)
Subjects: LCSH: Imposter phenomenon. | Self-doubt. | Professional employees—Psychology. | Career development.
Classification: LCC BF637.I46 S76 2023 | DDC 158.1—dc23/eng/20230501
LC record available at https://lccn.loc.gov/2023016030

ISBNs: 9781538724798 (hardcover), 9781538724811 (ebook)

Printed in the United States of America

LSC-C

Printing 1, 2023

For Leann:
extraordinary human and world's greatest cheerleader.
You are missed every day.

Contents

Contents

Acknowledgments

I'd like to start by thanking the many teachers, mentors, and colleagues who have contributed to my learning and growth in ACT and psychological flexibility. Without you, my life would have been very different—not just my career, but how I choose to live. There are far too many to name, but each one is a member of the Association for Contextual Behavioral Science, so I will thank the entire ACBS crew, members and staff alike. ACBS has been a better professional home than I ever could have imagined. I am so grateful for the ongoing learning and support I continue to receive from this incredible community. A panel I chaired on imposter "syndrome" at ACBS World Con was the spark that ignited the journey to this book.

My professional mission is to share the psychological flexibility skills that have allowed me to live this incredible life so that others might do the same. Thank you to those who have given me the platform to do so. My first publisher, New Harbinger, and acquisitions editor, Catharine Meyers, took a chance on this unknown wannabe author and let me publish my first two ACT books. It was my dream to grow as an author—one who could get a literary agent and publish with a Big Five publishing house. If it weren't for those first two books, this may never have happened.

Acknowledgments

Thank you to my agent, Jill Marsal, who saw my potential and the potential for this book even though I didn't have the world's biggest platform—and for making my agent and Big Five dream come true. Most days, I still can't believe it.

Thank you to my editor, Nana K. Twumasi. I adore working with you. You have that perfect editor blend of making a book better while maintaining the author's voice. I loved your questions, insights, and advice to go with my gut—you have no idea how many times that helped during the writing and editing process. You should also win an award for most responsive editor on the planet. Even when I didn't need you, I took so much comfort in knowing you would be there in a flash if I did. And thank you to the rest of the team at Balance, Grand Central, and Hachette. It truly takes a village to get the ideas and words of an author into the hands of actual readers.

Writing is a solitary endeavor, one where you can get so in the weeds your words sound like gibberish. I owe so much gratitude to my writing partners and brain trust: Yael, Debbie, Tamara, and Emily. Thank you for your thoughtful edits, unending encouragement, and always-valuable career advice.

Yael and Debbie—you are not just writing partners, but podcasting cohosts and cherished friends. Sometimes I still can't believe we've been together only twice IRL! I will be forever grateful for the opportunity to join *Psychologists Off the Clock*—it has been life changing in so many ways and is work that I find energizing, fulfilling, and deeply meaningful. I so value the collaborative and supportive nature of our relationships, and this book would not be what it is if not for you.

Michael Herold—thank you for inviting me to be a guest on the *Art of Charm* podcast to talk about imposterism. I sure felt like an imposter, but that experience was what led me to write this book. Thank you for your contribution to it and for being a bright light in this often-dark world.

Katy Rothfelder—thank you for helping this not-an-academic-anymore author access the research articles I needed and for your support during the early stages of book research.

Dad—you were my first model for choosing courage and living full-size, not fun-size. Thank you for always being there and for your advice, support, interest, and encouragement. You may be a WHMP, but I'm pretty sure I've turned you into a feminist too. I love you.

To my main squeeze, Billy—working from home with you these past two-plus years has been such a gift. I know I didn't always appreciate your pop-ins while I was writing, but I did appreciate your patience with my in-the-zone-induced irritability. Your tolerance, humor, thoughtfulness, and cleverness are my favorite. Thank you for your enthusiasm every time I shared a writing milestone. Love you, HB.

Scarlett and Liam (sorry, I mean William)—thanks for loving your mommy even when her psychological flexibility skills fall short. I promise I will keep trying harder every day.

Thank you to everyone who contributed their stories, including my clients who provided creative ideas for metaphors and exercises—allowing me to include your personal experiences and wisdom brought this book to life. It is a true honor.

And finally, thank you to my dear friend Leann Harris, whose bright light was extinguished far too soon. I was fortunate to be one of Leann's first book-coaching clients during her certification process with Author Accelerator. We talked, texted, and Zoomed often. She was my best cheerleader, making me believe I *had* to write this book even when my own imposter voice got loud. I am certain that were it not for Leann (and Jennie Nash's *Blueprint for a Book* and Jess Lahey's sample proposal, both provided by Leann via Author Accelerator), my agent and Big Five author dreams would not have come true. I'm pretty sure Leann was also pulling some strings from beyond.

Part I

UNDERSTANDING

Chapter 1

You Might Be a Fraud

The exaggerated esteem in which my lifework is held makes me feel very ill at ease. I feel compelled to think of myself as an involuntary swindler.

—Albert Einstein

You know that feeling—the one where you're *sure* at any moment your colleagues are going to find out you don't *really* know what you're doing, and you're not sure how you even made it to this level in your career? You tell yourself you just got lucky or the person who hired you must have made a mistake. Yeah, me too. I'm pretty sure the only reason I got into a competitive graduate school was because my dad knew the program director.

It started when a mentor in my psychology master's degree program suggested I apply to a PhD program at Boston University (BU) to work with David Barlow, a world-renowned anxiety expert. I hadn't yet heard of Dr. Barlow, but when I looked him up and saw the 1–2 percent acceptance rate at BU, I knew with 100 percent certainty I wouldn't get in. I'm not sure why I even applied.

I was living in San Diego at the time, but Boston was home. I grew up in a suburb about twenty miles west of the city (Natick—home of famed quarterback Doug Flutie and a Twinkie factory featured in an episode of *Family Guy*). I didn't tell my parents I had applied to BU, because I didn't want any pressure to come back home. Plus, what was the point when I wouldn't be accepted anyway?

Eventually, the secret ate away at me, and I confessed to my dad. "Dave Barlow?" he asked. "The psychologist?"

What? My dad was a business guy who knew nothing and no one in the field of mental health. Except, apparently, David Barlow. They belonged to the same golf club and had played together a few times.

The next time my dad ran into Dr. Barlow, he let him know I was applying to the program. Fast-forward a few months— miraculously, I was accepted.

I did well in the program and accumulated a number of successes after graduating. I started and still run a million-dollar business, I've published three books, I cohost a popular podcast with millions of downloads, I've done a TEDx talk, and I've presented to dozens of organizations. But to this day, over twenty years later, I still worry my dad is the only reason a mediocre applicant like me could have possibly gotten into a stellar program like that. In fact, I'm even worrying in this moment that when you read this, you will think, *Well, yeah, sure sounds like that's exactly what happened.*

If you've picked up this book, I'm guessing you can relate. Maybe you're in a position you're not sure you deserve. Or maybe you have professional dreams your brain has tried to usurp. *Who do you think you are?* it asks. *You're an amateur,* it chides. *You have nothing new or important or valuable to offer. You're a nobody. You'll never pull this off. You got this opportunity by chance or accident. You'll never be as good as the others. Any minute now you're going to be outed for the fraud you really are.* Am I getting close? If so, we are in the same club, my friend. In fact, deep down, the majority of successful people question their professional legitimacy a good amount of the time.

When I first decided I wanted to write this book, I was working with a book coach, Leann—because, you know, I couldn't possibly pull this thing off on my own, despite having pulled it off on my own two other times—and she asked me to write a one-page response to the question *Why do you* have *to write this book?* After reading my response, she asked, "Do you think of yourself as a psychologist who writes or a writer who's also a psychologist?" Damn, Leann. The truth was the latter, but the minute I admitted it, I was flooded with self-doubt and imposter feelings. I felt embarrassed, and my mind quickly said, *You are such a joke; you are not and never will be a* real *writer. You're a psychologist who is a* wannabe *writer.* It didn't matter that I had already been published. In fact, if I tried to make myself feel better by reminding myself of this, my brain answered with *Yeah, but those books were published by a small publisher and you didn't even have an agent, and your advance was tiny and they didn't exactly land on the bestseller lists.* Yikes.

Leann asked the question because she already knew the answer. Having found a passion for writing, especially as a vehicle to share evidence-based ideas from psychology to help people thrive (the very concepts I'm going to share with you in this book), I wanted it to become a larger part of my professional life. For that to work, I had to be good at it. I desperately *wanted* to be good at it. It mattered to me. Thus, enter the imposter.

If you look to the places where imposter syndrome shows up most for you, what you'll find in that very same spot is what matters to you. The voice that tells you you're not good enough, that you're a fraud, is doing so in an effort to protect you from failure and humiliation. It's also a big red neon arrow pointing out what is important—because if you didn't care, you wouldn't worry about being exposed as incompetent.

I am not an athlete. You know that saying "It's just like riding a bike," meaning once you know how to do it, you will always be able to do it? Well, when I got back on my bike after a decade of not riding, I immediately crashed. Yet I have never once worried about being exposed as an incompetent cyclist. Why? Because I simply don't care about my ability to pedal a two-wheeled vehicle. I do, however, worry about being exposed as a bad mother who hasn't yet taught her two kids to ride a bike, because I very much care about my role as a parent. Check your experience here. Where do you worry, and not worry, about being exposed as inadequate? How does this relate to what deeply matters to you?

Maybe it's possible to have these imposter thoughts and feelings and lean into your professional dreams without being bossed around by them.

I still have a raging case of imposterism. So if I'm not cured, who am I to be writing a book for other professionals who feel like imposters? Isn't that a little like trying to teach you how to be tall when I'm only five foot three? Maybe. But I'm also armed with a collection of psychology skills to outsmart imposterism. These are the exact tools I used to build my business, write and promote my books, do the TEDx talk, cohost my podcast, and give presentations to hundreds of people despite being filled with self-doubt and insecurity. This means that while I have a very loud and hypercritical imposter voice (I call her Sheila—we'll get to that later), I almost never let her win. Like Sy Sperling and his

Hair Club for Men, I'm not only the Imposter Club president—
I'm also a client (and child of the '80s).

THE IMPOSTER PHENOMENON

Just prior to the start of the 2020 COVID-19 pandemic, I had the
pleasure of participating in a writing retreat at the Kripalu Center for Yoga and Health. The bucolic campus was set on a lake in
the Berkshire Hills in western Massachusetts, and snow still lay in
patches on the ground despite the approach of spring. The dorm-
like rooms were adorned with twin beds and pink-tiled bath-
rooms straight out of the 1950s. I attended with my lifelong gal
pal Julie, a Harvard-trained architect who had been doing some
writing after losing her mother. On the first day of the retreat, we
sat in stiff armless chairs toward the back of the auditorium, having arrived too late to snag meditation cushions on the floor up
front. Playing the role of writer, I held my gel pen poised over my
notebook. The great Dani Shapiro sat cross-legged in an armchair,
center stage. Her presence and demeanor were calm, her voice
soothing and wise.

"How many of you are writers?" she asked, speaking into her
J.Lo-esque headset.

A sprinkling of hands lifted. Julie's and mine were not among
them.

"How many of you write?"

All two hundred hands reached for the stars. My chin dropped.
You too? I thought.

During a handful of breakout groups, I listened to the other
nonwriters-who-write read their writing. These were unpolished
responses to writing prompts, and they were *good*. This crew was

talented. And yet they didn't or couldn't see themselves as real writers. We were a bunch of frauds.

While I feel like an imposter as a writer, you may feel like a fraud when you consider going after a promotion or big-fish client, sharing your ideas in meetings, learning a new skill, working with more experienced colleagues, presenting at a conference, displaying your creative work, contemplating a career pivot or side hustle, or building a social media presence. There's no shortage of ways self-doubt can rear its ugly head, making you feel like an imposter.

But fret not. I'm going to share the collection of psychology tools I mentioned earlier to help you manage your imposter feelings in a whole new way. First, let's take a look at what the imposter phenomenon is, who is most likely to struggle with it, and how it develops.

The imposter phenomenon was first identified by Drs. Pauline Clance and Suzanne Imes in 1978 and later came to be known in pop culture as "imposter syndrome." In their original study of high-achieving women, Clance and Imes described the imposter phenomenon as "an internal experience of intellectual phoniness" that persists despite objective evidence to the contrary.[1] In other words, people who suffer from the imposter phenomenon are bright and successful but don't believe themselves to be despite their accomplishments. They question their legitimacy and whether they truly belong when they are part of an elite group. They believe others overestimate their competence,[2] and this causes a fear of being "found out" or exposed as a fraud.

The imposter phenomenon will affect up to 70 percent of us at some point in our lives. It was first thought to appear only in high-achieving women,[3] but it is now understood to be far more widespread, perhaps particularly so among marginalized groups.[4] Who are the lucky 30 percent who have never experienced it? Well, my dad for one, but we'll get to know him in a minute. Among the rest of the non-imposters are those guilty of a cognitive bias known as the Dunning-Kruger effect.[5] The Dunning-Kruger effect is a failure in self-awareness where people with limited competence wrongly overestimate their knowledge, skills, or abilities in a given area. Because these individuals are lacking competence, they lack the ability to recognize their own deficiencies and therefore don't seem to question whether they are legitimate or deserving of inclusion in a group. In other words, they're not smart enough to know they're not smart. Perhaps Charles Darwin put it best when he said, "Ignorance more frequently begets confidence than does knowledge."

My dad does not fall into this Dunning-Kruger group. He's both competent and (generally) self-aware. Bud, or Budsy, as my brother and I like to call him, is a seventy-five-year-old WHMP (pronounced "wimp," meaning white, heterosexual male of privilege— thank you, Dr. Janet Helms).[6] When I told Budsy I had chaired a conference panel on imposter syndrome, he said, "What? What the heck is that?" I went on to explain, thinking he'd recognize the phenomenon if not its name, but he remained utterly perplexed. He had zero experience of feeling like a fraud. This fascinated me. My dad is a successful entrepreneur. He started a company with a family of five to support while my mom stayed home with the kids. Fortunately, that company was profitable, but it never occurred to him that he might fail. He never had the thought *But I'm not an entrepreneur*, even though, with the exception of charging his fraternity brothers to use his steam bath in college, he'd never started or run a company.

In Western cultures, white, straight, cis, non-disabled boys are raised to believe they can do and be anything. They are invited to all the tables from the outset. Girls (especially those in larger bodies), BIPOC, members of the LGBTQIA+ community, immigrants, and disabled individuals have a history of being told they don't belong. For example, if you are Gen X like me, our mothers were brought up believing they could be teachers, secretaries, nurses, or mothers when they grew up. While my dad confidently started companies, never questioning whether it was his place to do so, his female contemporaries were likely experiencing the imposter phenomenon if they dared to venture into business, STEM, or other arenas not traditionally available to them.

The same may be true for those in other marginalized groups. For Black people, who were prohibited by law from occupying white spaces until 1965 (and who continue to be excluded due to racism today), imposter syndrome may be the rule rather than the exception. The Americans with Disabilities Act wasn't passed until the 1990s, and in many countries outside the US, accommodations remain abysmal. Homosexuality was deemed a mental illness until 1973 (a time when women still had to have male cosignatories on their credit card and bank account applications!). The World Health Organization removed trans* identification as a mental disorder only last year, and the American Psychiatric Association continues to include gender dysphoria in its *Diagnostic and Statistical Manual of Mental Disorders*. And one need look no farther than a current news outlet to see how half the country feels about immigrants. Any person from these disenfranchised groups who wishes to take a seat at a table that their not-so-distant history has suggested they are not meant to sit at may be more vulnerable to experiencing the imposter phenomenon.

Research on the role of race, gender, sexuality, and ability, however, is not entirely clear. Well-designed, scientifically rigorous studies are surprisingly lacking. In fact, while imposter syndrome is widely discussed in pop culture, with nearly 25 million results in a Google search, reputable research databases like PubMed return only about 150 results. Of the published studies on imposter syndrome, most have been simple correlational designs, teaching us nothing about cause and effect, and many have left out prevalence rates altogether.

To understand how uninformative correlations can be, let's say I told you there was a strong positive correlation between eating ice cream and drowning: the more ice cream people consume, the more people drown. Does this mean eating ice cream causes drowning? Nope. It just means both happen to occur more frequently in the summer. The correlation alone is truly meaningless. Imposter syndrome has been reported to correlate with certain mood states and personality traits. However, as in the ice cream example above, these correlations tell us very little and potentially open a door to inaccurate interpretations and assumptions. To avoid this, I will not be reporting the results of correlational research here.

A handful of studies have looked at imposter syndrome among racial minorities. One found that imposter feelings in university students were more strongly associated with mental health than was minority status stress.[7] Importantly, however, the main assessment tool used to identify imposter feelings was validated in primarily white samples. This means we can't confidently say the results accurately represent the nonwhite experience of imposter syndrome.

While some experts have suggested that women are more prone to experiencing the imposter phenomenon,[8] several studies have failed to demonstrate gender differences.[9] However, those studies did not look closely at marginalization. In other words, they did not split male-identifying participants into WHMPs and non-WHMPs. It is possible gender differences might emerge if only nonmarginalized men were used as the comparison group.

Still, cultural expectations around gender may be an important piece of the imposter puzzle. One study investigated the impact of performance feedback on both men and women reporting imposter feelings.[10] Men with imposter symptoms—who have been socialized to be competent and independent—reacted poorly when confronted with negative feedback. They displayed higher anxiety, lower effort, and poorer performance when held accountable to a higher authority. Women with imposter feelings—who have been socialized to be communal—demonstrated better effort and performance upon receiving negative feedback. So, while it remains unclear to what degree the *prevalence* of imposter syndrome varies by gender, when present, imposterism may *impact* men and women differently.

In my experience as a therapist, speaker, and podcaster who has worked and talked with many people about their experiences of imposter syndrome, those who identify as having a history of marginalization (which includes men from other-than-gender minority groups) appear more likely to experience the imposter phenomenon. Better research is needed, however, to really bear this out.

Ultimately, the imposter voice can arise for anyone in any context where they feel like an outsider. This might occur in a parenting or other family role (*I don't know what I'm doing; the moms have a better handle on this than us dads*), in a new role (*I'm just a newbie; I'm not a successful enough salesperson like these high-earning experts*), in a part-time or side-hustle role (*I'm not a real artist; I don't even support myself this way*), in a setting known for its competitive (academia) or youth (sports, technology) culture, or for a person who was accepted to a school as a legacy or through perceived nepotism or affirmative action (*I only got in because my sister went here / my dad knew the director / I'm a minority*).

Imposter "Syndrome"?

Though the imposter phenomenon was rebranded "imposter syndrome," some have recently argued this designation is problematic. Not only does the term pathologize a phenomenon that is nearly universal, but if my marginalization hypothesis is accurate, then those who experience it often do so because they have been victims of social oppression, not because they are living with a disordered psyche. The other argument against using the term *imposter syndrome* is that it places blame on individuals without accounting for the cultural context, and the focus becomes fixing individuals rather than fixing systems.[11] I couldn't agree more. And of course, if systems and organizations ever do get fixed, *many* things will change for the better. We'll talk about some ways to promote this change in chapter 12.

In the meantime, #thestruggleisreal, as the kids say (do the kids still say that? #imamiddleagedmom). If up to 70 percent of us struggle with imposterism, regardless of its origins, and the imposter experience is having a negative effect, it feels important to identify ways we can respond differently, at an individual level, while also working on organizational and systemic change. **That said, words and language have power, so for the remainder of the book, I will use the terms** *imposterism,* *the imposter voice,* *the imposter experience,* *imposter thoughts,* **and** *the imposter phenomenon,* **and not the more popular** *imposter syndrome.* **I hope you will consider joining me in this cultural rebranding too!**

IMPOSTERS BY DESIGN

As I was growing up, my parents called me "Tubby," "Little Tub-bette," and "Tubby Tubby Two-by-Four," presumably to prevent baby fat from becoming adult fat, which, predictably, had the opposite effect. My parents loved me and wanted what was best for me, but verbal and physical affection were rare—instead, top grades and other get-into-a-good-college achievements were what garnered praise. My physical appearance, by contrast, was a frequent source of critique. I would put on a skirt and gussy up my hair to get ready for an event, and my mom would ask, "Aren't you going to put a little blush on?" They put me on a diet when I was nine.

In response, I tried to people-please and achieve my way to love and acceptance. Around the time of that first diet, I started volunteering at school—I was a safety patrol officer and the standard-bearer in charge of our flag. I was so desperate for approval that I was willing to give a speech in front of hundreds of people at ten years old despite paralyzing fear. I got good grades and joined the choir. In middle school, I made the cheerleading squad. In high school, I was inducted into the National Honor Society and was voted president of the student council. I followed (most of) the rules and was *nice* and *polite* and *agreeable*, as girls are expected to be. Much of it garnered praise from my parents, but none of it was enough to dampen the criticisms about my appearance. In hindsight, I recognize these critiques came from their own insecurities, wanting to be good parents and for me to be OK in a harsh world. But that took time—and therapy—to fully understand.

Growing up being criticized for my appearance led me to develop an *I'm not good enough* story—specifically, *I'm not thin/pretty/acceptable/lovable enough*. Imposterism is an offshoot of this story—the fear that at any moment the truth of one's inadequacy will be revealed. Imposterism appears to develop from a complex interplay of early life experiences and evolutionary programming. Let's take a look at how imposterism may have taken root for you.

Early Life Experiences

As young people, we have a need to interpret and make sense of our experiences in a meaningful way. Efforts to do so result in the development of core beliefs or stories about ourselves, other people, the world, and the future.[12]

These stories develop early and stick. They mold themselves around whatever is going on in our lives. In high school, I thought, *Yes, I'm president of the student council, but if I mess anything up, everyone will know the truth about how unacceptable I really am.* Now, many years later, I think, *Yes, I've done a TEDx talk, but any minute they're all going to find out that I didn't really deserve it.*

If your parents had high expectations of you, but no matter what you did or how you did it, you never quite seemed able to please them, you likely cruise with an *I'm not good enough* story, joined by imposterism in your sidecar. So now you think about pursuing a professional goal and that internalized voice reminds you you're inadequate. Or maybe you're winning your tenth award and you still don't feel like you're enough, because no amount of achievement or success can erase your early experiences and the narratives that developed as a result.

Frustratingly, the opposite can also be true: if you had parents who offered abundant praise, you may experience the imposter phenomenon too. Perhaps your parents hooted and hollered for even the most benign of your so-called accomplishments. You went down the slide on your own? *Woo-hoo!* You zipped your sweatshirt? *You brilliant child!* You finger painted the toilet? *I'm not even mad—you might be the next Picasso!* This, too, can contribute to the development of self-doubt and imposterism. Why? Because you may have been small, but a part of you knew you didn't really deserve the praise. So now maybe you give an outstanding presentation—like standing-ovation brilliant—but dismiss any positive feedback as the audience "just being nice."

Unless we actually master the art of time travel, our early experiences are never going to change. The same is likely true of our self-stories. Much of pop psychology and most of the current books on imposterism would have you believe that the key to defeating the imposter voice is in changing your negative thoughts and believing in yourself as a professional. You've probably encountered a blog post or two with titles like "Five Tips for Thinking Positive Thoughts" or "How to Believe in Yourself." Not quite.

Unfortunately, old self-stories are pretty hardwired, and humans aren't manufactured with a delete button. Thankfully, there is an alternative, which I will share with you throughout part II. First, to understand how these narratives become so entrenched, we can look back a few hundred thousand years.

Evolutionary Programming

Unlike other mammals, early humans did not have sharp teeth or claws or the ability to run at high speeds. They had each other. Those who hunted, gathered, and traveled together had a survival advantage.[13] In this context, it was important for members of a group to frequently check themselves and their status: *Am I pulling my weight? Do I have value? Will my group keep me around, or am I at risk of being ousted?* What's more, dominance—being the best or the smartest or the strongest—made it more likely that genes would be passed on. Being exposed as less-than was a serious threat, so worrying about it in an effort to prevent it was adaptive. In other words, evolution programmed the fittest who survived to be prone to self-doubt, social comparison, and even the imposter experience. Today, being exposed as a mediocre accountant would not be a life-or-death situation, but our brains have not evolved to skillfully discern true threat from mere fret.

If you can't reprogram your evolutionary roots, change your early childhood experiences, or rewrite your self-stories, perhaps you're wondering how, then, you can ever hope to be more like the 30 percent who don't experience imposterism. It's one thing to escape it because you don't know any better (looking at you, Dunning-Kruger crew—who ironically don't know who you are and aren't reading this book); it's another to be smart and competent but just not question it (looking at you, Dad). Maybe you're thinking you need to learn to be more like Budsy. That to overcome imposterism, you can build your confidence and learn to stop questioning yourself. And maybe the way to do that is to just learn a little more about your industry, attend one more online course, read one more book about success, or get one more degree or certificate. Sound familiar? If so, you already know that won't work, because you've already tried it. Or perhaps more accurately, you're still trying it.

Here's what I know: there are no arrivals at *I did it—I'm a legitimate professional with zero doubts about my ability to perform well, be taken seriously, or pass everyone else's sniff test!* (unless you're a raging narcissist, perhaps, but then you definitely wouldn't be reading this book). There is only showing up to your work because doing so matters to you. The more something matters, the more you are apt to worry about being good at it. No matter how much praise you receive or how many goals you accomplish, you will not arrive at a place completely free of self-doubt or imposter feelings. Not even winning a Nobel Prize will do the trick, no matter how many times you tell yourself, *If I could just achieve this one thing, then I would finally feel legitimate.* There will always be something to trigger your self-doubt. Simply encountering another professional's brilliant work can send you back to *I'll never be* that *good.* My imposter voice gets the loudest when I'm learning new ideas from psychology or sharing them with the public, *because I care about it so damn much.* Taking courses from masterful trainers helps me better myself but also triggers *you'll never be* that *good* thinking.

We come by our imposter experiences honestly. Our brains were wired long ago to compare, and modern advances in technology have provided fertile ground to keep doing so. Social, cultural, and developmental experiences have impacted our vulnerability to feeling inadequate and imposter-y. So you see, if your career matters to you and you want to be successful, you can't escape these thoughts and feelings—and you probably won't ever get to change groups from the 70 percent to the 30 percent. In fact, as much as we'd like to believe the higher we climb, the more likely we are to chase away our imposterism, moving up the ladder means higher expectations. In other words, the CEO is expected to know and do more than the mailroom clerk. Thus, the imposter voice often *grows* rather than shrinks with success.

The good news is there are ways to respond to your difficult thoughts and feelings so they don't hold you back from going after the professional life you most deeply desire. I will show you the way, but first, we'll explore the different ways imposterism can play out.

The Recap: What to Know

- The imposter phenomenon is an experience of intellectual phoniness among high achievers who fear being exposed as incompetent frauds.
- Imposterism affects the majority of us, maybe most commonly those who have been marginalized, and is thus not a "syndrome."
- Many factors can contribute to the development of the imposter phenomenon, including evolution, sociocultural expectations, discrimination, and early learning experiences.

The Work: What to Do

In a journal, on your computer, or in the margins, answer the following:

- What are some examples of your own imposter experience? What does your mind tell you? What situations trigger the thoughts and feelings?
- In what ways have you been disenfranchised or marginalized? How may this have contributed to your experience of imposterism?
- What other kinds of early experiences may have influenced your experience of imposterism?

Chapter 2

What Type of Imposter Are You?

Have no fear of perfection—you'll never reach it.

—*Salvador Dalí*

At the risk of sounding like Captain Obvious, feeling like a fraud is the pits. No one *wants* to experience imposterism, and humans are quite talented at avoiding feelings they don't like (much more on this in chapters 9 and 10). In fact, we are so good at trying to dodge feelings of fraudulence that we overcompensate in an effort to prove our competence. The default set of strategies we use can be categorized into five subtypes of imposter. In this chapter, I'll share mine as well as those of four other successful professionals. Most importantly, you'll be able to identify yours.

In college, I took a creative writing class to satisfy an English requirement. I wrote a personal essay titled "Chicken Again," about my family's experience during a challenging time. I was never one of those kids who kept a diary or journal, so this was the first time I had written anything personal or painful, and it helped me process the experience.

I got an A- on the essay and in the class. I remember the professor discouraging my use of capital *S*s and *H*s when using female pronouns to identify my mother, calling the choice "too gimmicky." Why did this stick with me? I don't remember a single other college assignment, grade, or piece of feedback. Looking back, I realize I always wanted to write but something stopped me from believing the option was available to me.

I was already three years into college as a psychology major when I took that writing class. Back in high school, we had selected a handful of electives. My two favorites were Introduction to Law with the formidable Ms. McDade, who drilled into us that "ignorance of the law is no excuse," and Introduction to Psychology with Mr. Lawson, who once told my parents during a parent-teacher conference that I was a scatterbrain (which prompted my mother to buy me *Little Miss Scatterbrain* T-shirts and books for years). Despite Mr. Lawson's unfavorable critique, I fell head over heels in love with psychology. I was fascinated by what made people tick. I knew at sixteen that I wanted to be either a psychologist or a lawyer. After one summer internship at a boys' club law firm where men ruled and female colleagues were treated like second-class citizens, the psychology deal was sealed.

For the next fourteen years, I marched along the educational path that culminated in a PhD and a psychology license. All of this involved writing, but despite completing a master's thesis and a doctoral dissertation and publishing various book chapters and peer-reviewed journal articles, I never thought of myself as a writer.

I loved psychology and I was good at it, but scientific writing always felt like an unenjoyable chore, something other people were better at. I focused my career on therapy and teaching instead of research and writing. In fact, writing, especially creative writing, was something I never even thought about.

And then I had an idea for a psychology book.

This book idea had nothing to do with wanting to write (consciously, anyway)—it was a *professional* book, not a creative one. Practitioners of acceptance and commitment therapy (ACT) use many metaphors and experiential exercises in clinical work with clients. At the time, scripts for these practices were scattered throughout many different ACT books. One day, while I was sitting in my campus office, prepping an ACT lesson, I thought, *Wouldn't it be nice if I could just pull one book off my shelf, flip to a section on acceptance, and choose from a variety of appropriate metaphors and exercises?* It seemed so obvious, but it didn't exist. Yet.

In the next beat, I thought, *Maybe I should* write *that book?* This thought was immediately followed by *Who the hell do you think you are? You're not a writer! You don't know anything about writing books. You're not even an ACT expert! The ego on you to think you know enough to write a book about ACT!*

I was tempted to let that voice stop me in my tracks completely. I knew the only way to ensure I wouldn't humiliate myself was to just ignore the idea and go about my business. But I *knew* it was a promising concept. I just didn't know whether I had any place writing it. So I turned to others who I saw as more-worthy experts. I reached out to a former-mentor-turned-colleague/friend who was an ACT expert. She hadn't written a book either, but in my mind, she was legitimate—at the very least, she had adequate knowledge about the subject that I didn't believe I had. Together, we turned to her former mentor, Dr. Steven Hayes, who had written many books and is the originator of ACT. We asked for advice and sample book proposals, which he provided. Dr. Hayes also happened to be on the board of a small publishing house, so he couriered our proposal to the appropriate people, and lo and behold, we got a contract.

I had never felt more clueless or more like a fraud. Not only did I know nothing about book writing and not enough about ACT, but I believed we got a contract only because we happened to have that connection to Steve Hayes. I asked two former mentors, both book authors (one of whom had a husband who worked in the publishing industry), to look over the contract. My coauthor and I split up the chapters but asked other professionals to write the challenging chapter on theory. We relied on our editors. I told my husband, "If I *ever* tell you I want to write another book again, remind me of this moment where I am telling you I *never* want to write another book ever again!" I hated feeling like such an amateur and needing help from so many people.

When all was said and done, it felt good to have a finished book. We showed up to the one book signing our publisher coordinated at an ACT conference (and somehow the book managed to do fairly well despite my complete lack of publishing industry and marketing knowledge). I took a break from writing. I was done. I meant it when I said I never wanted to write another book.

Then my family went through a dark time, and I needed an outlet to process it. I wanted to return to creative writing. I stumbled upon a podcast called *Writing Class Radio*, about "the heart and art"—or story and craft—of writing narrative nonfiction. I listened to one episode and was hooked. I went back through the archives and binged two years of episodes. I started taking writing classes and reconnected with that feeling I had had when I wrote "Chicken Again." I started reading books about writing. I wasn't finishing pieces, sending queries, or trying to get published, but I was learning. I decided the reason writing *The Big Book of ACT Metaphors* was so painful was that *I just didn't know enough*.[1] I just needed a little more knowledge and experience, and *then* I would stop feeling like such an imposter. Then I could do—and share—the writing.

Over the next four years, I took five writing classes, attended one writing retreat, joined a writing group, started a writing group, went to two writing conferences, read seven books about writing, listened to five writing podcasts (not episodes, but full seasons), followed writers and editors on social media, subscribed to three writers' newsletters, read countless articles on book launches and platforms, and hired a book launch consultant, marketing consultant, branding firm, and book coach.

I wrote another book, but I also spent nearly $20,000.

Why? Because I am an Expert Imposter.

THE IMPOSTER SUBTYPES

In her book, *The Secret Thoughts of Successful Women: Why Capable People Suffer from the Impostor Syndrome and How to Thrive in Spite of It*, Valerie Young suggests that people with imposterism develop distorted ideas about what is required to demonstrate competence.[2] These competencies fall into five categories: the Expert, the Perfectionist, the Soloist, the Natural Genius, and the Superhuman.

The Expert

Expert Imposters believe their competence is measured by how much knowledge, skill, expertise, and experience they have—and they never feel they have quite enough. There is always one more degree, course, credential, book, article, or expert to consult. This may be particularly prevalent among those from marginalized groups who have been told they have to be twice as good or know twice as much to measure up to those in the dominant group.

Expert Imposters struggle with uncertainty—they often don't

take things on unless they're *sure* they can deliver. For example, an Expert Imposter wouldn't apply for a job or promotion unless they knew they met every qualification (and then some). The costs of being an Expert Imposter are many: stagnation for those who keep learning but never really *do* the thing they set out to do, self-silencing for those who fail to express themselves out of fear they might be exposed as unknowledgeable, and as you saw in my case, fiscal handicapping due to the high costs of classes, degrees, and conferences that are meant to fill the Expert's cup of knowledge. Only this cup has a hole in its bottom, and no matter how much is poured into it, the cup is never topped off.

Importantly, this is not to say that skill building or learning about an industry is inherently problematic. But Expert Imposters often don't know where to draw the line between learning and doing.

The Perfectionist

Jamil was born in Tanzania. When he was four, his parents divorced, and his mother won custody of him and his brother, an unlikely outcome for African Muslims. She moved the boys to England so they could pursue higher-quality educational opportunities. When Jamil was thirteen, his mother was diagnosed with terminal cancer. Because she was a single mother and did not want to send her boys back to Africa to live with their biological father, she asked a close family friend to adopt them. This meant a second immigration to the United States, where Jamil spent his adolescence raised by an affluent white family on the Upper East Side of New York City.

Jamil never felt special, but he did feel different. In England,

25

he had lived in a diverse immigrant community. But when he moved to New York with his British accent, dark skin, and more formal new family, he started to question where and whether he fit in.

Jamil's adoptive parents recognized his intelligence and encouraged him to apply to Phillips Academy Andover, a prestigious boarding school in Massachusetts. Jamil's educational path took him from Andover to Stanford undergraduate and then on to medical school, where he hoped to focus on global health in both the US and Africa. Following his internship and residency at Emory University, Jamil went on to Harvard for his fellowship. He rose up the ranks to medical director of Children's National Hospital and associate professor of pediatric and emergency medicine at George Washington University. His fourteen-page CV is truly something to behold.

Despite Jamil's impressive achievements, he didn't always feel self-assured about his competence or belongingness. Starting at Andover, where every student was high achieving and most were white, he realized he had to raise his game to keep up. He also became aware that people saw his skin color first, and he felt he had to ace everything to prove his competence. Around the time he was applying to colleges, affirmative action became controversial. He questioned whether he deserved the placements he achieved or whether he was "just given a spot" due to his race or because his adoptive family was wealthy. He told me he spent his early career chasing prestigious appointments, thinking, "If I graduate from there, no one will doubt me."

To prove his competence, Jamil set extremely high standards for himself, and in many ways, his standards helped him succeed. But he never raised his hand unless he was 100 percent certain he knew the correct answer, and he applied only for jobs he knew he was more than qualified for. When assignments were due, he completed them well ahead of time, then perseverated on every detail to make sure everything was just right. When he had to speak publicly, he spent copious amounts of time rehearsing. He worried that mistakes would reflect poorly not only on him but on the Black community as a whole. Instead of pursuing global health, he found himself on an achievement ladder, chasing what others thought were the best, most prestigious career moves.

Jamil is the Perfectionist Imposter.

Perfectionist Imposters have a laser focus on one thing: getting things done flawlessly. They believe nothing short of perfect is acceptable and they must deliver an unblemished product or performance at all times. Perfectionist Imposters are convinced there is a right and wrong way to do everything, and they can sometimes be as critical of others who fail to measure up to their high standards as they are of themselves. While perfectionism can help the Perfectionist Imposter achieve, it also has a number of drawbacks. Perfectionist Imposters struggle to delegate tasks, believing if they want something done right, they are better off doing it themselves. This means always having too many things on the to-do list and rarely having enough time to do them all, especially at the high level they demand. To avoid mistakes or possible failure, which leads to feeling incompetent, Perfectionist Imposters sometimes avoid new or challenging tasks, risking stagnation and even boredom. For some Perfectionist Imposters, when they do things extremely well, they rarely feel pride or satisfaction, instead thinking about the things they could have done better. For others, including Jamil, doing things well may leave them feeling pleased with themselves, but this also reinforces the need to continue working harder and harder.

The Soloist

As a child growing up in Germany, Michael was diagnosed with a progressive muscular condition that ultimately required the use of a wheelchair. Knowing he had little control over the deterioration of his body led him to feel the need to compensate by proving himself academically and professionally. His university entrance exam scores were superior and got him into a competitive computer science program, where he developed a love for film animation. He was accepted to a film school in the United States and was offered a job working on a popular 3D animated picture before he even completed the program. After fifteen years working in animation (always thinking, *They are going to figure out they hired the wrong guy; give it two weeks and they will kick me out*), he realized he'd met his goals, but something felt lacking. He decided to pursue a career in self-development as a way to help young adults living with disabilities. He began speaking publicly and gave a powerful and inspiring TEDx talk.[3] He ultimately landed a job with the Art of Charm, an exceedingly popular self-development/coaching organization and podcast. For Michael, the thought *Who do you think you are?* showed up a lot along the way. He often felt the need to mention his training and other professional achievements to colleagues and clients out of fear they might question his competence.

While Michael was internally motivated, without much need for praise or props, he also held himself to very high standards, often taking on numerous extra responsibilities as a way to prove himself capable of doing anything and everything. He not only felt the need to do everything perfectly (he jokes this is because he's German) but also felt he must do it all on his own.

In his mind, not knowing the answer and needing to ask for help exposed him as a fraud. "I dread the day I have to say, 'I don't know,'" he told me.

Michael is a Soloist Imposter.

For the Soloist Imposter, to be competent means being able to succeed without any help from others; accomplishments count only if they're achieved on one's own. Soloist Imposters can struggle with collaboration because goals they meet as part of a team diminish their feelings of success. If a Soloist needs to ask for assistance, they feel vulnerable and weak, seeing this as a sign they don't really know what they're doing, and therefore confirming they're a fraud. Soloists often end up taking on the workloads of three people even if it costs them their health or diminishes the quality of their work product. When the Soloist Imposter manages to succeed on their own, they rarely feel satisfied or accomplished, instead thinking they got away with a secret—that they're actually barely managing to keep it together.

The Natural Genius

Alanna was the first person in her Indigenous Canadian family to pursue higher education. She sailed through her undergraduate and master's degree programs and was offered a job at one of the largest and most prestigious consulting firms right out of graduate school. She excelled as a consultant in various capacities but ultimately was left feeling uninspired. Alanna knew she loved two things: wine and music. So despite knowing nothing about the industry or how to run a business, she became a certified sommelier and opened a wine bar and music venue—it quickly became one of the most popular hot spots in her city. In this role, Alanna's eyes were opened to the repercussions a lack of access to medical and mental healthcare can have on people who are in need, especially members of marginalized populations. She was inspired to pivot and pursue her lifelong dream of attending medical school.

Med school was a whole new ball game for Alanna. She was used to things coming easily to her—success had not required excessive study in the past. Now, being a student who was considerably older than her peers and realizing she would not be able to skate through like she had before, Alanna felt like an imposter. To her, success was a product of natural ability. Because medical school was difficult for her, she surmised she did not possess the natural ability to be a doctor and therefore was a fraud and a failure.

Alanna is a Natural Genius Imposter.

The Natural Genius Imposter believes that intelligence and ability are innate qualities that lead to effortless success. For the Natural Genius, competence means being able to excel with ease and speed. Natural Genius Imposters believe they should be able to hear or learn things once and understand them completely. The Natural Genius wants to get it right the first time—struggling to immediately grasp something offers confirmation they are a fraud. There are parallels between this and Carol Dweck's well-known concept of *fixed mindset*.[4] Both Natural Genius Imposters and those with a fixed mindset often have trouble persevering through setbacks, because they believe they just don't have what it takes, and they see little value in putting in the effort to learn. This is because the Natural Genius believes you either have it or you don't—and when you don't, it confirms you're a fraud. This may lead to avoidance of challenges in an effort to circumvent failure. When Natural Genius Imposters succeed, their confidence enjoys a boost, but this is often short lived, as any setbacks cause their self-esteem to suffer.

The Superhuman

Janina emigrated from Ukraine at age twelve, after living through the Chernobyl nuclear disaster and enduring significant discrimination for her Jewish heritage. When she arrived in the United States, she spoke no English and was suffering from the aftereffects of Chernobyl radiation. To make matters even harder, her family did not accept her LGBTQIA+ identity.

By age thirty-seven, Janina had earned two PhDs, published ten books, contributed to fourteen more, created and hosted three podcasts, participated in countless panels as an expert in psychology and pop culture, and delivered two impactful TEDx talks,[5] all while still experiencing migraines and seizures caused by the early radiation exposure. Nonetheless, the day before her first TEDx talk aired, Janina had eighteen panic attacks—all before lunch. Afterward, she rewatched the video of her talk over and over, hunting for mistakes, ripping herself to shreds. Sound like the Perfectionist? It is. And then some.

Janina is the Superhuman Imposter.

According to Valerie Young, the psychologist who identified the five subtypes, the Superhuman is the Perfectionist, the Natural Genius, and the Soloist "on steroids."[6] In addition to her many other roles, Janina worked for me as a psychologist in my anxiety clinic. She carried double the caseload most others would be capable of managing. If you needed a clinical consult, she was the first to volunteer. If you were sick, she offered to bring you soup and Gatorade. She remembered your kids' birthdays and your wedding anniversary. She rarely said no to requests and almost never asked for help (she pretty much never asked for anything).

She did all these things because she is genuinely one of the most kindhearted, compassionate humans you will ever meet. Her desire to help is deep and real. But there is a dark side. When Janina says no, sets limits, or asks for help, she feels like a fraud and a failure.

Superhuman Imposters believe that competence means being able to juggle all the balls—even if the balls are on fire—while also balancing on a unicycle, singing show tunes, and smiling. How expertly the balls are juggled definitely matters (that's the Perfectionist part), but being able to handle All the Things, all the time, is what distinguishes the Superhuman from other imposter subtypes.

Janina has pushed herself to the point of collapse to avoid feeling like a fraud. The thing is, all Superhumans eventually try to juggle one flaming ball too many, and when the balls come tumbling down, this reinforces the belief that the Superhuman is incompetent. Even when the Superhuman is delivering a flawless juggling unicyclist performance, they rarely feel satisfied, because their mind says they should be able to add spinning plates on sticks balanced on their face. *If I were really competent, I could do it all easily and without help.*

COMMONALITIES

After I interviewed Jamil, Michael, Alanna, and Janina and reflected on my own experiences, I realized we all had some important things in common: our imposter feelings grew out of early experiences of marginalization and often kicked into overdrive as soon as we set our sights on doing something that held true *meaning* for us. Jamil first noticed imposterism when he applied to colleges that he believed were the path to global health and when he realized his choices might reflect on his larger Black and African communities. Michael and Alanna talked about shifting careers because they wanted to make a difference and do something with purpose. Janina and I experienced imposterism during our psychology graduate programs, but these feelings were amplified when we pivoted toward writing, creating, and speaking in earnest.

When did imposterism kick in for you? How have experiences of marginalization or meaning played a role?

There is a way to cultivate your dream career even if you recognize yourself in one or more of these imposter subtypes. Most people see themselves in multiple subtypes (and the subtypes do share some overlap) but find one to be the most dominant. To determine yours, head to the "Take the Quizzes" section of my website (www.jillstoddard.com/quizzes), and respond to the brief questionnaire. Part II of this book will show you how to successfully pursue the professional life you most deeply desire. Unfortunately, part II is not a prescription for how to cure your imposterism—because there is no cure. But while there may not be a cure, there *is* psychological flexibility, which is about to become your new superpower.

The Recap: What to Know

- There are five subtypes of imposter: the Expert, the Perfectionist, the Soloist, the Natural Genius, and the Superhuman.
- Each imposter type relies on a different set of strategies to prove competence; these strategies may appear to stave off imposter feelings in the short term, but they ultimately backfire.
- You can identify your subtype at www.jillstoddard .com/quizzes.

The Work: What to Do

In a journal, on your computer, or in the margins, jot down the following:

- Your imposter subtype
- The ways in which you attempt to prove your competence based on your subtype
- How this "works" and how it backfires

Chapter 3

There Is No Cure
(but There Is an Alternative)

I have written eleven books, but each time I think, "Uh oh, they're going to find out now. I've run a game on everybody, and they're going to find me out."

—Maya Angelou

I had an idea for a panel discussion to be presented at a professional conference I attend every year. I wanted to gather successful, prominent women to talk about their experiences with imposter syndrome (this was before I understood we should stop calling it a "syndrome"). Mostly, I wanted to demonstrate how we had all used ACT to live boldly, in spite of feeling like imposters, in hopes that it would inspire others to do the same. I got Dr. Janina Scarlet, whom you read about in the last chapter; Dr. Lisa Coyne, a prolific author and president of the professional organization hosting the conference; Dr. Miranda Morris, a successful entrepreneur and the president-elect; and Dr. Debbie Sorensen, Harvard PhD and cofounder and cohost of our *Psychologists Off the Clock* podcast, to participate on the panel. What followed was one of the most powerful conference experiences I've ever had. These women opened up to hundreds of attendees, on camera (the conference was virtual), and tearfully shared their stories of feeling deeply inadequate. The audience response was overwhelming. Most of the feedback sounded something like *I can't believe even you feel this way—if you can feel it and still go after big things that matter to you, maybe I can too.* Mission accomplished.

Shortly after the conference, I received an email from the *Art of Charm* podcast. The hosts were interested in having me on as a guest to talk about imposter syndrome. I had not yet met Michael (you also met him in the previous chapter; he works at the Art of Charm) nor heard of the show, and I had no idea how they'd found me. According to the invitation, their past guests included Kobe Bryant, Dan Harris, Gretchen Rubin, Adam Grant, and Sugar Ray Leonard. At the time, they had over *a hundred million* downloads.

As I read the email invitation, my heart raced and my face burned. My imposter voice kicked in: *This must be a mistake. Or a scam. How do they even know me? I'm nobody. I'm certainly no expert on imposter syndrome. I'm not sure I should do this. What if I do it and they figure out I don't really know as much as they think I know?*

It turns out the Art of Charm found me through the conference panel. Michael had attended and was so taken by the talk that he suggested me as a guest. I was the moderator of the panel and spoke for only the first ten minutes, introducing the concept of the imposter phenomenon and talking about the five subtypes you read about in chapter 2. I could see why Michael thought I knew my stuff, but those facts all came from other people's work. Of course, this made me *really* feel like an imposter. *The Art of Charm should be interviewing* them, *not me.*

Despite the raging fear and self-doubt, I said yes to the invitation. I wasn't an expert in imposter syndrome (yet!). But I had a PhD in clinical psychology from a top program, and I *was* an expert in anxiety, which is certainly part of imposterism, and ACT, the therapy I used to help my clients and readers with their imposter experiences. I also cohosted a podcast and had been a guest on about fifteen other podcasts to discuss my book *Be Mighty*, so I knew a thing or two in the podcast domain as well. In other words, *I knew enough, even if I didn't know everything.* At the very least, I knew how to prepare for an interview to be able to discuss the topic intelligently for an hour. But not a PhD, not fifteen other podcast appearances, not expertise in anxiety and ACT, and not cohosting a popular podcast of my own were enough to cure my imposter fears.

During the interview, one of the podcast hosts was asking about the 30 percent of the population who do not experience imposterism. I joked that Donald Trump was a perfect example. When I listened to the episode, they had cut the part about Trump. Now, rationally, I can understand they did this as a way to ensure none of their listeners would be offended. With such a huge audience, a portion was bound to be Trump supporters, even if I was not. But the primal part of my brain that represents the part of me who doesn't want to be kicked out of the club ruminated on that one aspect, to the exclusion of the rest of the interview, like a skipping vinyl record. Those thoughts sounded like *See, I knew I couldn't hang with a hundred-million-downloads podcast. I should have known better.*

Once that record stopped skipping, my brain started to worry that I had focused too much on women and minorities when their audience was probably predominantly white men. A new skipping record took over: *Why didn't you ask who their audience was? You're such an amateur. You should have prepared better.*

At one point, I asked Michael how many downloads the episode had, in case I wanted to include it in some pitches I was putting together. He said something like "About sixty thousand in the first week, which is a respectable number." I latched on to the word *respectable*, combined with his tone, which my brain turned into *Your episode was pathetic and unpopular, and I regret that I took a chance on you.* Later, Michael told me my episode was the *Art of Charm*'s fifth most popular in 2020. *Art of Charm* is a weekly podcast, so that means my episode was in the top 10 percent. My rational mind can say, *Hey, top 10 percent, not too shabby.* My inner imposter still wishes I could have a do-over.

IMPOSTERISM AND SUCCESS

Imposterism is common among high-achieving individuals and may even be correlated with success.[1] The irony is, the more we achieve, the more we may be prone to experiencing imposterism. If you look at your personal history, it may be like an Escher painting—climbing the achievement ladder seems to put you farther from the top, or farther from feeling like you've made it. On the one hand, this makes no sense. Shouldn't adding to our portfolios or CVs systematically chip away at the fear of being found out? If we're gaining more knowledge and experience as we rack up accomplishments, it would stand to reason that we ought to feel less fraudulent.

On the other hand, it makes perfect sense. The higher we climb, the more we are expected to know. If you've never run an organization, you're allowed to not know everything about being its president. But if you're the HPIC (head person in charge), you'd better be up to speed! Now the amount you know as a higher-up, which may not feel vastly greater than what you knew when you started, doesn't count for as much, and you are expected to know more and more as you continue to rise up the ranks. And, as imposterism expert Valerie Young puts it, "success only makes it worse because now you have a reputation to defend."[2]

While it has been theorized that imposter experiences may worsen with success, the actual research on the relationship between success and imposterism is not entirely clear. Whether imposterism improves, stays the same, or worsens with success seems to depend on a number of contextual factors. For example, men are more likely to have their workplace experiences and leadership style validated over time,[3] ultimately improving confidence and reducing self-doubt. Women, especially mothers, queer women, women of color, and women living with disabilities, are more likely to have their competence, contributions, and leadership style questioned repeatedly over time.[4] This likely erodes confidence and causes professional women to question their success despite their accomplishments. Interestingly, girls and women who attend non-coed institutions and Black students who attend historically Black colleges report higher levels of confidence than those attending coed or racially diverse schools, respectively.[5] Jamil, the physician you met in chapter 2, told me his imposterism improved with success. He attributed this to learning and working in academic and professional environments where the dominant messages were *This is a prestigious place; if you're here, you deserve to be here.*

THE CYCLE OF IMPOSTERISM

Experiences trigger feelings—some we like, some we don't—and whether we want to have more or less of those feelings will impact how we behave; how we behave will in turn impact how we feel. Psychologists refer to this as "reinforcement learning." We can begin to understand how imposter feelings may grow even as we rack up achievements by looking through a lens of positive and negative reinforcement learning.

To begin, I want to clarify a common misconception about terms, especially the term *negative reinforcement*. I often hear people refer to a parent yelling at a kid as an example of negative reinforcement. As in, "He yelled at his kid, and it made her act out more because negative attention is better than no attention." This is actually an example of positive reinforcement. The words *positive* and *negative* do not refer to *pleasant* and *unpleasant*, respectively. They indicate whether something is being added (positive) or taken away (negative). *Reinforcement* means *a consequence that leads to an increase in behavior*. So in the example above, if adding attention (even if it's angry yelling) increases unwanted behavior, it is an example of positive reinforcement. If the yelling "works" to decrease the behavior, it would be an example of positive punishment—adding yelling (positive) decreases a behavior (punishment).

Parents may have an easy time imagining this: your kid is having a tantrum in the grocery store because they want candy. They are loud and you're embarrassed, so you just give them the darn candy. Voilà—tantrum ends; everyone is happy. The next time you're in the store, do you think your child will be more or less likely to throw a tantrum? Do you think *you* will be more or less likely to give them what they want? Both are more likely. Giving your child the candy they want is an example of positive reinforcement of *their* behavior, because you are adding something (candy) that increases the likelihood the behavior (having a

tantrum) will occur again. It is also an example of negative reinforcement of *your* behavior—taking something away (the loud,
embarrassing tantrum) makes the likelihood you will do the same
thing next time (give them the candy) more likely.

Positive and negative reinforcement can explain a lot of our
behavior. Why do you procrastinate, for example? Giving yourself
permission to put off an aversive task *removes* (negative) feelings
of dread or anxiety, and that relief increases the likelihood (reinforcement) you will procrastinate again the next time you have an
aversive task at hand. Of course, the removal of dread and anxiety
is only temporary, because you still have the same task waiting to
be completed, possibly with less time to do so (if it's a task with a
deadline). This ultimately increases dread and anxiety. Whatever
shall you do now? Well, one thing you've learned from experience is that procrastination "works"—the last time you tried it,
the dread and anxiety went away for a bit, so now you're more
likely to do it again.

Drinking alcohol, taking drugs, shopping, gambling, and
overeating can all be understood through a lens of both positive
and negative reinforcement: something is being added (dopamine
or other "feel good" chemicals or neurotransmitters) *and* something is being subtracted (boredom, anxiety, or another difficult
internal experience). This double reinforcement whammy makes it
easy to see why behavior change is so hard!

We can begin to understand imposterism in a similar way.
Some people respond to imposter feelings by jumping on a ham-
ster wheel of constant achievement. Others respond to imposter
feelings by avoiding challenging tasks. These seemingly opposite
behaviors can both be understood through reinforcement learning.

Achievements, like getting another degree or taking on a promotion, add something (pride, satisfaction, a feeling of competence) that increases the likelihood we will keep achieving (positive reinforcement), while also temporarily subtracting feelings of inadequacy or fraudulence that will also increase the likelihood we will keep achieving (negative reinforcement). In other words, the more we move on up, the more we *need* to move on up in an effort to feel better. The cycle looks something like this:

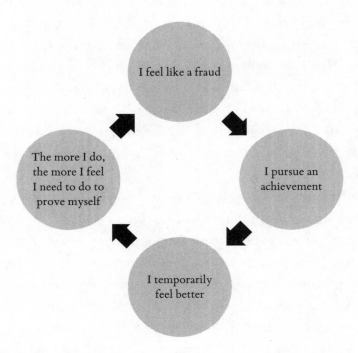

Likewise, *avoiding* challenging tasks that trigger fears of being exposed as a fraud temporarily removes feelings of self-doubt and anxiety (negative), increasing the likelihood we will continue to avoid taking on new challenges (reinforcement). That cycle looks like this:

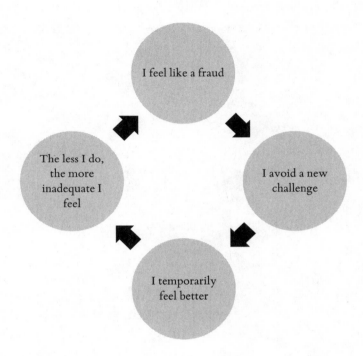

We can break this down further as a way to understand the subtypes from chapter 2. Let's take a look at the Expert, the Perfectionist, the Soloist, the Natural Genius, and the Superhuman.

Consider how this fits for you. Are you trying to "fix" imposter feelings in ways that make you feel better in the moment but actually maintain the cycle? Are you avoiding new challenges, overachieving, or both?

The Expert

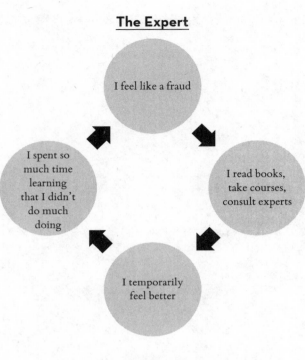

The Perfectionist

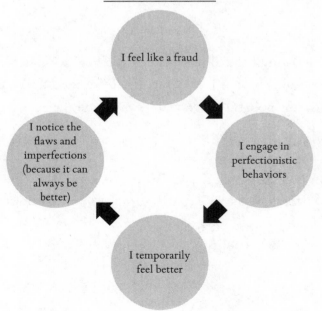

The Soloist

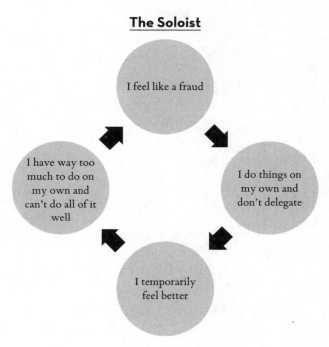

The Natural Genius

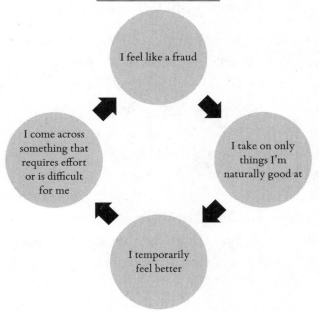

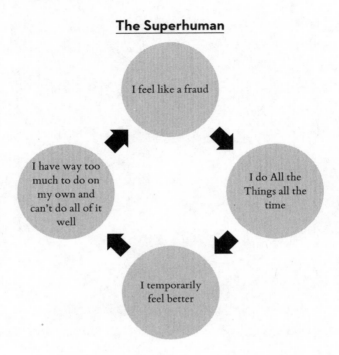

The Superhuman

Is Imposterism Really So Bad?

The cycles demonstrate that the more we achieve or avoid, the more we need to achieve or avoid. Avoidance of new challenges has a clear downside—growth is sacrificed, and stagnation takes its place. But is stacking up accomplishments because we feel like imposters really so bad? In his latest book, *Why Do So Many Incompetent Men Become Leaders? (And How to Fix It)*, Tomas Chamorro-Premuzic argues that many of the world's top leaders are high achievers because they are their own worst critics, and it is their relentless pursuit of excellence that motivates them to close the gap between where they think they are and where they want to be.[6] We might not have their contributions if it weren't for a little imposterism.

MIT professor Basima Tewfik argues the imposter phenomenon is not uniformly detrimental. In a well-designed series of studies, she found that high-achieving individuals with a greater frequency of imposter thoughts were more interpersonally effective[7] and sometimes demonstrated greater job mastery.[8] So it appears achievement and imposterism *can* have benefits. Tewfik's mentor, the well-known organizational psychologist Adam Grant, argues that feeling like an imposter may have three specific benefits:[9]

1. It can motivate us to work harder, because we feel like we have something to prove.
2. It can motivate us to work smarter, because it causes us to doubt and then rethink our strategies.
3. It can make us better learners and leaders, because doubt leads us to seek ideas and second opinions from others.

However, Tewfik notes the mechanism through which imposter thoughts have beneficial outcomes is a *defense mechanism*. In other words, individuals who fear being exposed as incompetent attempt to salvage their diminished sense of self-worth by taking an other-focused approach. (*I feel anxious about my lack of competence, so I will compensate by being likable instead.*)

Breaking the Cycle Through Psychological Flexibility

So are imposterism and achievements good things, or problems? *It depends.* It depends what your behavior is in the service of. Are you pursuing degrees, promotions, recognitions, and other achievements only in service of chasing away your imposterism? Do you say yes to writing one more paper or giving one more talk because you think this is the step that will finally elevate you to feeling competent and legitimate? Are you overly focused on what others think, and is achieving more and more an attempt to bolster your self-esteem by impressing those you believe are evaluating you? Or are you achieving because you care about pursuing bold action—what Tara Mohr calls *playing big*.[10] I think of it as living full-size as opposed to fun-size—you know, like candy bars? On Halloween, everyone knows the house that gives out full-size candy bars (and there's usually only one, if any at all). Full-size is exciting, sometimes surprising or unexpected, and maybe even a little forbidden.

I said yes to the *Art of Charm* podcast *not* because I thought it would finally cure my imposterism (and PS: it didn't) but because I wanted to embrace living full-size. My approach to this book is much the same. Truth be told, even as I work on it, there's a now familiar hum in the background: *Who are you to write this book?* The voice is constant. But writing this book matters to me. Sharing science-backed ideas to help people thrive is my professional mission. So even though I have no idea how the book will be received (and I'm afraid no one will read it or like it), I choose to write it anyway in service of choosing a full-size professional life.

When I talk about living full-size, what I'm really talking about is *psychological flexibility*. Psychological flexibility refers to our ability to show up to each present moment fully—aware of and open to all our thoughts, emotions, physical sensations, and urges—and to make conscious, deliberate decisions to do what deeply matters to us.[11]

Over the past several years, research demonstrating that psychological flexibility is one of the strongest predictors of overall health and well-being has exploded. Those who are more flexible have better functioning related to mood, anxiety, panic, body image, weight management, interpersonal relationships, chronic pain, acute pain, migraine, cancer, smoking cessation, psychosis, tinnitus, and more.[12] *Psychologically inflexible* is what we are when we hide, running on autopilot, in our comfort zones (or when we enact our defense mechanisms). The comfort zone isn't so bad sometimes. Rest is important. And who doesn't like spending a night on the sofa with a warm cup of tea, a cozy blanket, and their favorite TV program instead of having to be "on" at a conference or professional networking event? But the comfort zone is never where the magic happens. It is certainly not the place from which we grow.

Importantly, psychological flexibility is all about *choice*. Each present moment offers an opportunity to choose. If you are consciously choosing the comfort zone as a form of values-based self-care rather than a way to hide from pain, that is psychologically flexible.

So what's the verdict? Is racking up achievements good or bad? *It depends.* It depends on whether you are going after something in a psychologically flexible way (going big, even when you feel fear and self-doubt, in service of something that matters to you) or in an inflexible way (overachieving in an attempt to cure or outrun imposterism).

RULES ARE MEANT TO BE BROKEN

Psychological inflexibility stems from language.[13] Specifically, an overreliance on language and the things we say to ourselves—things like rules, reasons, rationalizations, assumptions, judgments, and predictions—to the exclusion of direct personal experience. Let me tell you a little story about Twitter. You know the place: where doom scrolling both satisfies an itch and simultaneously makes you hate everything. It's one of the many places creative professionals are supposed to hang out to "build their platforms." Ugh. I was writing my Twitter bio when I thought, *Put "author"*— quickly followed by *What?! You're not an* author. *You can't say that.* But, reader, I was signing up for Twitter because I was preparing for an upcoming *book launch.* For my *second book.*

In this example, my mind was telling me (i.e., language) I couldn't write "author" in my bio, because I was a fraud who was not a real writer. But there was nothing in my experience to support this assertion. The fear that I would be called out was simply a story I was telling myself (story = language). When I did put "author" in my bio, guess how many Twitter police officers came after me? Exactly zero. But we all know there are trolls on the internet who find our most sensitive buttons and push them, and my mind also had a story about how catastrophic that would be and how ill equipped I would be to handle it. This was the *cognitive negativity bias* in full effect.[14] That is, we humans are hardwired to overestimate threat and underestimate our ability to cope. This served a useful function for prehistoric humans, who had to outrun killer kangaroos, but it isn't so necessary in our modern age. Still, neuroimaging studies show that our brains light up and get active far more around negative emotions (like fear, anger, disgust, and sadness) than around positive ones (like happiness).[15] But you know what my experience tells me? I've gotten a bad book review or two, and here I am, still standing and still writing. My mind might say *Stop! Don't risk it!* but my experience tells me the bad stuff typically doesn't occur, and even if it does, it's not so terrible and I can cope with it.

Our minds are miraculously adept at trying to protect us from humiliating ourselves or being rejected or failing. They tell us we are imposters and frauds on the verge of being found out so that we act in ways to prevent this dreaded outcome from occurring. But when we listen to their warnings as if they are Truths with a capital *T*, either we give up a full-size life and end up living fun-size—which isn't actually fun at all—or we bend over backward trying to prove ourselves and end up burned out and miserable. We also never allow our experience to show our minds how wrong they can be, that (1) the catastrophes are never as frequent as our minds predict, (2) even when they occur, they are typically not as bad as our minds imagine, and (3) we can handle them far more effectively than our minds assume. Predictions, imaginings, assumptions—these are all examples of "languaging" that gets us stuck.

When our minds get going—you know those dreadful spirals they're so fond of?—we typically have feelings, both emotional and physical, that are as painful as the stories themselves. I don't know about you, but I'd rather not feel scared shitless or full of doubt. Attempts to avoid those difficult feelings at the cost of pursuing what really matters to us also create psychological inflexibility. Basically, in moments of choice, when we listen to our minds and run from our feelings in the service of avoiding a feared outcome, without giving thought to the person we most deeply desire to be or the life we most wish to live, we are being psychologically inflexible. We are living fun-size, not full-size.

Think of a goal, a dream, or an aspiration you have (or had and gave up). If I say, "Take one concrete step today to move in the direction of making that happen," what comes up for you? How do you feel physically and emotionally? What does your mind tell you? Maybe it says you don't have what it takes yet, and you should put it off a bit longer until you know more and feel confident. Maybe it says if you take one step, you must go all in, and you're not sure you're ready for *all that*. Whatever shows up, your answers are your first clues about how language—rules, reasons, rationalizations, assumptions, judgments, predictions—and a desire to avoid discomfort might be keeping you stuck. Our minds and bodies can be obnoxiously compelling.

What you are going to learn in the upcoming chapters is how to change your *relationship* with these internal experiences (thoughts, emotions, physical sensations, urges) so they no longer get in the way of you having the career (and life) you want. What you are not going to learn is how to change, control, or reduce the internal experiences themselves. This is not a book about positive thinking, curing anxiety, eliminating self-doubt, believing in yourself, or building self-esteem and confidence. If I had the key to all of that, I promise I'd share it with you, but it's simply not how things work. And remember, psychological flexibility is about being aware of and open to *all* internal experiences, fully and without defense—meaning we are in the business not of changing our experiences but of allowing them to be as they already are. We will talk much more about this in chapter 9. The reason I mention it here is to try to be clear about what it means to be psychologically flexible, as building psychological flexibility is the entire purpose of this book. Plus, I'm guessing you've already tried to think positively and improve your self-esteem and confidence and it hasn't exactly worked.

You're not alone, and you're not doing it wrong. Previous

psychological advice that has suggested the only path to success is via changing our thoughts and feelings is now outdated. Contemporary research has found this doesn't work and often backfires.[16] In part II, which is coming up next, you'll learn a new science-backed way of relating to internal experiences so they no longer hold you back. I have been cultivating psychological flexibility in my own life for twenty years, and I am certain it is what has allowed me to thrive even when things felt impossible or soul crushing. The first step is through expanding your awareness of what is getting in your way.

The Recap: What to Know
- There is no achieving your way out of imposterism: the higher you climb, the more you're expected to know.
- Imposterism is maintained by a cycle of reinforcement learning.
- We can break the cycle by becoming more psychologically flexible—opening up to all internal experiences and making choices based on values.
- Psychological inflexibility occurs when we get hooked by language and avoid discomfort.
- We don't need to change our thoughts and feelings; we need to change our relationship with them.

The Work: What to Do
In a journal, on your computer, or in the margins, jot down the following:
- Your imposter cycle (with or without your subtype).
- Examples of your own psychological inflexibility: What feelings (emotions, sensations, urges) do you most tend to avoid? In what ways has listening to rules, reasons, rationalizations, assumptions, judgments, or predictions kept you stuck (either avoiding or overworking)?

Part II

EVOLVING

Chapter 4

Getting off Autopilot: The Gift of Presence

Freedom is the individual's capacity to know that he is the determined one, to pause between stimulus and response and thus to throw his weight, however slight it may be, on the side of one particular response among several possible ones.

—*Rollo May*

There's a deleted scene from the movie *Pulp Fiction* where Mia Wallace asks Vincent Vega, "Do you listen or wait to talk?" Vincent answers, "I have to admit that I wait to talk, but I'm trying harder to listen." Say what you will about Tarantino's movies—the man knows how to write dialogue. Tarantino wrote this scene with his finger on the pulse of human behavior. If we're being honest, aren't we all a little Vincent Vega? Instead of being dialed in to the present moment, we're thinking ahead to what's next. Later, we go over every detail of the conversation, beating ourselves up for what we did or didn't say. We miss the moment because we time travel into the future and past.

The ability to cognitively rewind and fast-forward is uniquely human and can be helpful. Remembering yesterday's construction traffic will prevent you from being late today when you choose an alternate route. Thinking ahead to next week's project deadline will help ensure your deliverables are produced on time. But this is also another place where language can lead to psychological inflexibility. Ruminating about the hurt you experienced in your last relationship may lead you to shut down in your next (or avoid relationships altogether), even if connection and intimacy matter to you. Worrying you could be exposed as an incompetent fraud if you pivot to a new field may keep your feet rooted to the spot, resulting in stagnation even if professional growth is something you deeply value.

So how do we weigh and balance the benefits and dangers of cognitive time travel? Via *awareness* and *choice*.

MAY I HAVE YOUR ATTENTION PLEASE?

Humans make an estimated thirty-five thousand decisions on any given day,[1] the great majority of which occur on autopilot.[2] Thank the stars above for autopilot. Can you imagine if we had to think through thirty-five *thousand* choices every day? Our ability to pay attention to the endless barrage of sensory inputs in our environment is limited in capacity and duration, so our brains were designed to be picky.[3] The cognitive process of *selective attention* allows us to focus on a particular stimulus while filtering out irrelevant details. In this way, you can read attentively on the train while ignoring the sights, sounds, and motions of other passengers.

Various models of selective attention exist. Some suggest we scan for and zoom in on what matters,[4] while others propose we filter out what doesn't.[5] While this ability keeps us from being overstimulated, it can also rob us of meaningful or joyful experiences when the brain decides what's important based on language.

When we wrongfully interpret (interpretations = language) a context as dangerous (either physically or socially), our attention is pulled to the perceived threat, to the exclusion of other things.[6] This, of course, keeps us safe when the threat is real. An armed robber barges into the bank? Hit the deck. Who cares how beautiful the ceiling art is or what perfume the teller is wearing? But what if the threat isn't actually a threat?

In her Netflix special, *The Call to Courage*, Brené Brown tells a story about an afternoon she went for a swim with her husband, Steve, while on vacation at Lake Travis.[7] She was totally dialed in to the present moment and shared with Steve that she felt deeply connected to him. His response? "Yeah, water's good." She detected a threat. Her mind generated some language-y reasons her husband was "blowing her off": she was aging, her body was unattractive, and he was no longer into her.

Having learned a thing or two during her years as a shame and vulnerability researcher, Brené handled this beautifully by observing her thoughts, sitting with her feelings, and choosing an openhearted conversation. But based on her experience from years past, she shared from the Netflix stage how she *would have* responded had she been on autopilot, reacting from a place of perceived threat. She described it like this:

"I will go into complete pissed-off mode. I will beat him back to the dock, fueled by nothing but rage and fury. He'll go 'Hey, babe, what's for breakfast?' and I'll say [in a sarcastic tone], 'I don't know, babe—let me ask the breakfast fairy...Oh, I'm sorry, Steve. I forgot how vacation works: I'm in charge of breakfast and lunch and dinner and packing and unpacking and laundry and sunscreen and towels and bug spray.'"

When Steve said, "Yeah, water's good," Brené perceived a

threat—she believed her husband was rejecting her, and she felt fear, loneliness, and shame. But her interpretation was wrong. It turns out Steve wasn't rejecting or judging Brené at all; he was just hyperfocused on his own internal experience of threat. He shared with her that he had been fighting off a panic attack that had been triggered by some language-y stories of his own—he had been worrying about being an inadequate protector. Steve's response to Brené had had nothing to do with her! They had separately gotten hooked by their minds' stories and hijacked by shame.

In the absence of *awareness* of these internal experiences, a space to choose a values-consistent response does not exist. Instead, there is just raw autopilot reacting.

Brené circumvented the breakfast-fairy confrontation using a defusion technique (more on this in chapter 8) she calls her "magic sentence." Whenever Brené is caught in assumptions, predictions, or other unhelpful language, she says, "The story I'm telling myself is . . ." Paying mindful attention to her internal experiences broadens her awareness and provides her the space to make a more conscious decision about how to proceed, rather than simply reacting.

What we're talking about here is the first major building block to developing psychological flexibility: mindfulness. Mindfulness refers to our ability to pay attention in a particular way: on purpose, to the present, and without judgment.[8] Mindfulness has been studied extensively in recent years. Mindfulness-based practices have been shown to reduce stress,[9] blood pressure,[10] distress, anxiety, depression, rumination,[11] chronic pain,[12] symptoms of psoriasis,[13] symptoms of fibromyalgia,[14] symptoms of ADHD,[15] burnout among healthcare professionals,[16] and more.

Mindfulness programs have also begun to permeate the workplace. Google, Aetna, the US Army, and graduate programs at

Harvard and UC Berkeley are just a few of the organizations that have implemented formal mindfulness training programs for staff and students.[17] Research investigating the benefits of mindfulness at work has found improvements in social relationships, resilience, performance,[18] commitment,[19] and emotional exhaustion.[20] Richard J. Davidson and colleagues found those in particularly high-stress jobs experienced improvements in mood, energy level, and immune functioning following formal mindfulness training.[21]

While seated or guided meditations are one way to practice being more mindful, they are by no means the only way and are not what we will be focusing on here. The way I think of mindfulness is like the time between a detonator being pushed and a bomb exploding. Here's what I mean.

The Bomb Metaphor

Picture a detonator, a fuse, and a bomb. The length of the fuse determines how long it will take for the bomb to explode once the detonator has been pushed. When we're reacting on autopilot (excuse the now mixed metaphor), rather than thoughtfully and deliberately choosing from a place of awareness, the fuse is minuscule: the detonator gets pushed; the bomb goes off. Lots of things can push our detonators—rejection (perceived or otherwise), negative feedback, parenting challenges, traffic, global pandemics, stress, anxiety, uncertainty, and of course, language—including imposter thoughts.

Criticism is a big detonator pusher for me. My bomb often explodes quickly in the form of me reacting defensively, without considering the type of person (partner, colleague, supervisor, etc.) I wish to be in that moment—one who is open, receptive, curious, and humble. Becoming more mindful—aware of the present moment, including our thoughts, emotions, physical sensations, and urges, in a nonjudgmental way—serves to lengthen the fuse. In the space created, we can tune in to how we wish to respond, rather than simply reacting based on how we're thinking and feeling. As we go along, the skills you'll acquire will help make deactivating the bomb a much easier task. But first, mindfulness *creates the space* in which we can practice those skills and choose a new response.

Making Sense

My favorite way to get present is by using my senses. Take a minute, right now, to close your eyes and just listen. Really listen. I have music playing (David Gray—one of my favorites). But when I close my eyes and really listen, I hear my clock ticking, my dog snoring, and my stomach gurgling—all noises I wasn't aware of before. Now choose any nearby object and look at it. If you're somehow in a space completely devoid of objects, just look at your hand. Really look. Notice the details.

Notice, too, if your mind wanders. Maybe the sound of your air-conditioning reminded you of a trip you took to Oregon last year when the temperatures reached an unimaginable 115 degrees. Then maybe your mind wondered when you'd be able to visit Oregon again and when would be the best time to experience more-typical Pacific Northwest weather. And now maybe you're worrying about the future impact of climate change. Whoa, there goes that wandering, time-traveling brain!

Also notice the mind's tendency to judge. Maybe your mind labeled the traffic sounds "annoying," or the freckles on your hand "ugly." If your mind is wandering or judging, that doesn't mean you're doing mindfulness wrong. While the definition of *mindfulness* includes "present-focused" and "without judgment," remaining present 100 percent of the time and erasing judgments is utterly impossible. However, if you can catch when your mind has wandered or judged, let those thoughts pass, and gently redirect your attention back to the present, focusing on the objective qualities you are hearing or seeing, you are being mindful. It is an ongoing process of returning to the present and letting go of judgments over and over again. Practice in this moment by carefully observing smell, taste, and touch. For real fun, try writing with your nondominant hand.

If you're wondering how producing something that looks like a four-year-old wrote it will help with imposterism, it won't. Not directly, anyway. But it will help you build your mindfulness muscle. If you set a goal to climb Mount Everest when you haven't even hiked the flat trail behind the neighborhood park, you're not going to head out to Nepal this weekend or even this year. You're going to train. A lot. Similarly, if you have any hope of getting skilled at dismantling your bombs, you can't just read a definition of *mindfulness* and magically stop reacting. You have to train. A lot.

Using your senses to stay present and let go of judgments is an attentional practice. I want you to get good at noticing. As you become a better observer of what you see, hear, smell, taste, and touch, you will be better equipped to notice what you're thinking and feeling. Expanding your awareness (a.k.a. lengthening the fuse) of the thoughts and feelings that push your detonators (or arise when external triggers push them) positions you to thoughtfully choose your response rather than having your bomb explode. But that's Everest. So first, we train.

Mindful Eating

Here's some guidance for building your mindfulness muscle using an eating exercise that includes practice with all five of your senses.

- Choose a food you like.
- Hold it in the palm of your hand. Really **look** at it: color, shape, light, shadow, etc. (sight).
- Bring it to your nose and **smell** deeply (smell).
- Place it in your mouth but don't bite. Roll it around and notice how it **feels** in your mouth and on your tongue (touch).
- Notice any changes in saliva or an urge to bite.
- Chew. Notice how this **feels** (touch). Notice how this **sounds** (hearing). Notice the **taste** and changes in your mouth (taste).
- Notice the urge or desire to swallow (but don't swallow yet).
- Swallow, and notice each aspect of this experience.
- Notice judgments and evaluations (they will likely be positive if you chose a food you like).
- Repeat with a food you dislike.

PAIN × PRESENCE = FREEDOM

When I was a kid in the early 1980s, I hated PE (or "gym," as we used to call it). Thanks to JFK's Youth Fitness Program, my tight-polyester-shorts-clad gym teacher, Mr. Francoise, would make us do calisthenics while playing a record called "Chicken Fat," the theme song for the JFK program. The lyrics, by Meredith Wilson, commanded kids to do push-ups every morning (not just once in a while!), referred to "flabby guys," and called the listener "chicken fat."[22]

Because I was a bit of a chubby kid and my parents called me "tubby," doing jumping jacks while listening to "Chicken Fat" was, needless to say, not my favorite. In third grade we had a combined gym class with the fourth graders. My class was lined up on one side of the gym, directly across from and facing the big kids on the other side. At one point, I really had to use the bathroom. I raised my hand and kept it raised, but Mr. Francoise would not call on me. Being a "good girl" who followed the rules, it never occurred to me to jump out of line and approach him (or just run straight to the bathroom!); I was too afraid I'd get in trouble. Eventually my little eight-year-old bladder couldn't take it any longer, and the next thing I knew, I was standing in a puddle, my formerly light green Healthtex slacks now dark green in just the wrong places. I was humiliated.

I was never going to be a world-class athlete, but up until that point, I'd enjoyed physical activity as much as the next elementary school kid. In middle school, puberty, combined with group changing rooms, turned gym class into a nightmare. I didn't have the upper-body strength to climb the ropes or to complete the bent-arm hang during the Presidential Physical Fitness Test (and the only time I ever cheated at anything in my life was when I terminated that mile run a lap early). By age twelve, I had developed an intense loathing for exercise.

When I began exercising as an adult, every step-aerobics class, weight-lifting session, treadmill walk or jog, or stationary-bike ride was accompanied by thoughts like *This sucks. I hate this so much. I'm sweating my ass off. I can't breathe. When will this be over? My legs are tired. I don't get how people actually enjoy exercise. This is miserable. I'm so bad at this. I'll never be able to maintain this as a habit.*

Screw everyone who makes me think I need to do this to get skinnier. Judgment, judgment, and more judgment.

When I learned about mindfulness, I started to apply the practice while exercising. I noticed the feelings in my muscles *without judgment*. I observed my breath as it entered and exited my body—its rate, rhythm, and sound—*without judgment*. I got curious about all the parts of my body that moved in tandem *without judgment*. And something kind of miraculous unfolded. No, I did not fall head over heels in love with exercise and sign up for an Ironman event. But I stopped hating it quite so much. Exercise became just that: exercise. Rather than being all the things my mind said about it. Exercise on its own came with some pain. But exercise + judgment + judgment + judgment created a whole new level of suffering.

In Buddhism they say pain × resistance = suffering. Judgment is a form of resistance. Tara Brach tells us pain × presence = freedom.[23] I love that. We don't escape being human without a generous helping of pain. But sometimes we get to choose how much we suffer. Being present with our experiences while letting go of judgment reduces suffering and offers freedom.

Showing up for small meaningful moments, even amid a life thick with painful experiences, also reduces suffering. At the height of the COVID-19 pandemic, my colleague Hank Robb shared a metaphor about lemons that I just loved and have since adapted and extended to illustrate the importance of showing up and being present for these moments as a way to reduce suffering and create freedom.

Lemons

They say when life hands you lemons, make lemonade. But they don't tell you how to make lemonade if you don't have any sugar.

I don't know about you, but it seems like the sugar has been pretty sparse these last couple of years with global pandemics, climate change, school shootings, and all the rest. If we've been able to avoid squirting the juice in our eyes, we're batting a thousand (again, apologies for the mixed metaphors, but you get what I'm saying). When life gets lemony, it can feel next to impossible to find the sugar. It can also feel like being present while enduring all the sour and sticky is the last thing we want to do. But here's what I know: the only way to experience sweetness is to show up. To show up for the small, seemingly insignificant moments. This is how we make lemonade, however slowly, one granule of sugar at a time. Maybe it's taking your first sip of coffee in the morning, feeling the warmth of the sun on your skin, experiencing a rare moment of your children cooperating when they don't know you're listening, being greeted by your dog when you arrive home, getting a simple text from someone you care about, hitting all the green lights on your way to work, or sharing a smooch with your partner. These things won't erase all the other tiny annoyances we experience the rest of the time. They won't eradicate social injustice or save the planet. They won't make going after the career you deeply desire any less intimidating. But they will add that little bit of sweetness we all deserve and balance out the sour we can't avoid.

Many of us live in cultures where we've been taught that life is about the big moments: graduations, job promotions, bonuses, awards, weddings, babies, vacations. But if we're lucky, we maybe get a dozen or so of these in a several-decades-long existence. So what is the rest of life? Really, isn't it mostly the small moments strung together over time, with a few biggies sprinkled in? If we miss the small moments, we miss life.

In their book *Life Lessons: Two Experts on Death and Dying Teach*

Us About the Mysteries of Life and Living, Elisabeth Kübler-Ross and David Kessler teach us the lesson of time: that time is not promised to any of us, so we need to learn to be present while we're here.[24] A big part of building a meaningful personal and professional life is being present (nonjudgmentally) for all our moments, big and small. Another is being clear about why it matters.

The Recap: What to Know

- Mindfulness is the process of paying attention to the present moment in a deliberate, flexible, and nonjudgmental way.
- Mindfulness creates space between triggers and reactions. In this space, a more conscious choice about how to act (either persisting or desisting in behavior) can be made.
- Mindfulness can be practiced as a formal meditation or simply by tuning in to sensory experiences.
- Mindfulness—formal or informal—has many benefits.
- Showing up and being present for the small moments matters.

The Work: What to Do

- Practice strengthening your mindfulness muscle by seeing, hearing, smelling, touching, and tasting in a present-focused, curious, nonjudgmental way.

Chapter 5

Keep Your Why Close By: Getting Clear on What It's All For

*I have learned that as long as I hold fast to my beliefs and values—
and follow my own moral compass—then the only expectations I
need to live up to are my own.*

—*Michelle Obama*

I attended high school from 1987 to 1991, when Duke University's basketball team consistently appeared in the Final Four tournament and Christian Laettner and Mike Krzyzewski were household names. I didn't give a whale's tail about basketball, but I imagined myself being part of a student body that celebrated its team's domination as a cohesive community of diehard fans. I toured the Duke campus and fell in love with the neo-Gothic and Georgian architecture. I felt in my bones it was where I belonged. Duke was a "reach school" based on my SAT scores and lack of AP courses, but I graduated from high school in the top 5 percent of my class and had tons of extracurricular activities and leadership experiences, so I thought maybe I had a chance.

I thought wrong. I was rejected from my dream school.

This would be the first of many failures, from additional school rejections to podcast pitch rejections to crickets when trying to build a social media presence to hiring a couple of nightmare staff members to writing children's books and personal essays for ten years without a single publication.

The average five-to-eighteen-year-old's educational path involves minimal choice: attending school is the law, and public schools don't require applications, so there is nothing to be rejected. After high school, applying for a first job, trade school, or university is one of the first big choices we make as we venture into our professional lives. It's exciting and scary and hopeful and intimidating. With choice (and applications), we encounter a vulnerability that didn't exist in quite the same way before. The stakes feel higher, the threat of rejection more pronounced. Sure, maybe as a younger kid you got picked last for kickball in PE, didn't get the lead in the school play, or had your prom invite declined. Some rejections begin early in life—I see this with my own kids feeling hurt by elementary school friends leaving them out of a game or not inviting them to a birthday party. But kids seem to bounce back better and faster from these experiences of pain. How do they keep going socially even after they've been hurt? What do they have that adults seem to lose along the way?

This is a complicated question, and although a complete answer isn't currently available, some research suggests we may be more psychologically flexible as kids, and this flexibility diminishes over time as the complexities of language we discussed in chapter 3 begin to fully take hold.[1] But before that, kids feel their feelings and have their thoughts and choose to put themselves back out there *because connecting with friends and having fun are important to them.*

Earlier, I shared some of my experiences with writing—how the Expert Imposter in me spent an immense amount of time and money trying to learn the industry and craft so I would feel less like a fraud. What I didn't mention was how I continued to write for *ten years* despite many manuscript rejections. Maybe you're thinking I should have stepped away from the keyboard—that surely ten years of regular rejection was a sign that I was a lousy writer. But to me, what really mattered was *why* I kept writing, not the *outcome* of that writing. Of course, I wanted a specific outcome—to get published—yet whether I achieved that goal or not did not dictate whether I chose to write.

VALUES: YOUR WHY

In the last chapter we talked about mindfulness as the first building block to psychological flexibility. Mindfulness creates the space between a trigger (like a rejection or failure leading to imposterism) and a response (like stepping away from the keyboard) so that we might make choices based on something other than uncomfortable feelings or self-critical thoughts. That "something other" is our *values*. Our values are our why.

Values are what we want to be about in our lives. They are what we want to stand for, who and how we wish to be as we navigate this one life. They represent what truly matters to us. They are how we are living when we are living a meaningful life.[2] A life centered around values is a life freer from suffering. Research has found that reductions in both pain and avoidance don't lead to increases in meaningful living, but increases in values-consistent living do result in decreased struggle and suffering.[3] We can start to unpack your values by thinking about them in a three-tiered cone, wide side up, point down.

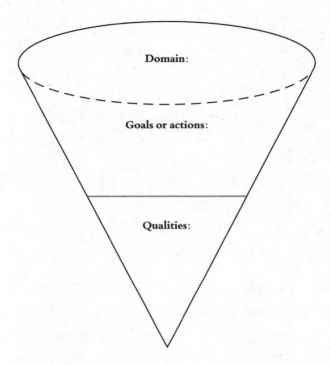

The top layer represents domains of living. These are broad categories like friendship, marriage, parenting, career, education, extended family, health, spirituality, recreation, community, and service.

The second tier is what we do. It represents goals we might have or actions we might take within each of these domains. This might include things like finding a more fulfilling job, spending time with your family, or practicing better self-care.

Like the bottom of a snow cone, the third tier is where the juicy stuff resides. This tier represents what I really mean when I say *values*. This tier includes the *qualities you wish to embody* as you engage in the actions from tier two, under the domains in tier one. While tier two represents what you do, tier three represents *how* you do it. This might include qualities like being loving, attentive, present, thoughtful, bold, brave, persistent, compassionate, or self-respecting.

List of Common Values

Accepting	Faithful	Persistent
Adventurous	Fit	Playful
Affectionate	Flexible	Present
Assertive	Forgiving	Reliable
Attentive	Free	Respectful
Authentic	Friendly	(of self and/or
Autonomous	Genuine	others)
Bold	Giving	Responsible
Brave	Grateful	Romantic
Caring	Helpful	Sensual
Committed	Honest	Sexual
Compassionate	Humble	Silly
(toward self	Humorous	Skillful
and/or others)	Independent	Spiritual
Contributing	Industrious	Supportive
Cooperative	Just	Thoughtful
Courageous	Kind	Tolerant
Courteous	Knowledgeable	Trusting
Creative	Loving	Trustworthy
Curious	Loyal	Virtuous
Dependable	Nurturing	Wealthy
Exploratory	Open	Willing
Fair	Orderly	

Engaging in the actions from tier two in the absence of embodying the qualities in tier three is not valued living. Take the example of spending more time with your family (or friends or partner, etc.). Let's say you commit to getting together every Sunday night for dinner. If you're scrolling through social media, checking email, or taking calls throughout the evening, you may be showing up, but consider *how* you're doing so. If you care about family (tier one: domain) and you commit to spending more time with your parents, siblings, kids, or cousins (tier two: actions/goals), the most important variable in the values equation is *how* you show up (tier three: qualities). Are you distracted? Or do you choose to show up as an attentive sibling, playful parent, or present cousin?

Or perhaps you have a goal in tier two to get a promotion or, in my case, publish an essay. If you fail to achieve your goal, feel like an imposter, and are not deeply connected to your third tier—perhaps qualities like perseverance, courage, skillfulness, or creativity—you may be more likely to quit even if the goal matters to you. To stick with your goals, you might ask yourself, *Why does this promotion matter to me? What kind of person do I most deeply want to be, and how can I continue to be that person even if I feel like a fraud and don't get this particular position?*

I write because I want to be a person who embodies creativity, challenge, learning, skill building, courage, and persistence. So I keep trying even when my work is rejected and I feel like an imposter. After ten years of rejections, I published my first essay in year eleven. You might consider how to use your values to make the promotion more likely next time. And if it still doesn't happen, you can keep embodying those values in an intentional way to keep going in directions that matter to you. Importantly, bear in mind that we don't control most outcomes, only the steps we take in hopes of achieving them (more on this in chapter 6). Taken together, these three tiers represent your why.

Before we dig deeper into your values, let's see if you can start with some brainstorming about what your cones might look like. Use a different cone for each domain, following the example below.

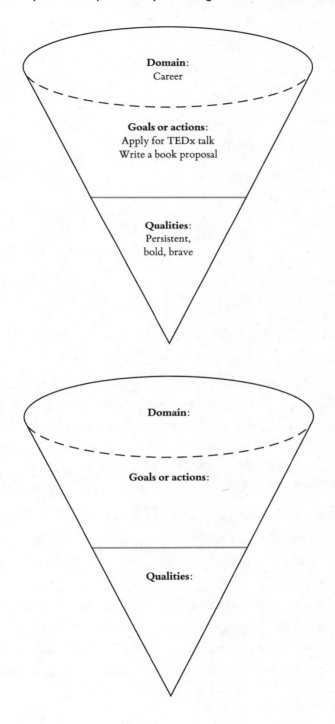

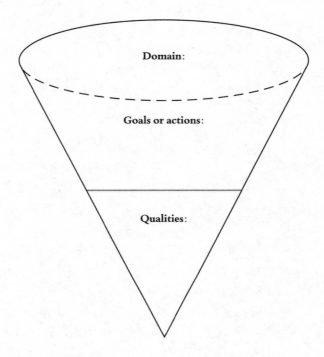

If you're feeling uncertain after completing a cone or two, not to worry—we have much more to unpack. Let's start by clarifying a few important points regarding what values are and are not.

Values Are...

Values represent the Me you most deeply desire to be as you choose actions that matter and bring meaning. Broken down a bit more, values are also freely chosen, ongoing, and moves toward something.

Values are freely chosen. This means values are not "shoulds," nor are they chosen by your parents, religion, friends, culture, or any other community. Your values may align with your parents, religion, culture, etc., but what is important is that they have been chosen by *you* in the absence of external pressure or prescribed rules or regulations. In fact, when your values are not freely chosen, you may become vulnerable to what psychologist Jack Brehm calls "psychological reactance," or the tendency to act in the opposite direction when external expectations create a sense of threat to your experience of freedom.[4] Essentially, your inner adolescent rebels, even when this comes at great personal cost.

Values are ongoing. You are never "done" with a value. Unlike a goal, which has an end point or can be checked off a to-do list, values are qualities we embody in an ongoing way. You will never achieve the status of perfectly affectionate partner, supportive colleague, or assertive employee. Affection, support, and assertiveness are qualities we choose to return to again and again. We are never finished being affectionate, supportive, or assertive.

Values are moves toward something. When you engage in valued action, you are moving toward the person you want to be and the life you want to live. This may be comfortable or uncomfortable. You are not moving away from something you don't want to have or feel. For example, you might value being helpful. A "being helpful" move toward will be intrinsically rewarding (even if it involves sacrifice), like working at a soup kitchen on Thanksgiving because you wish to pay it forward. An example of a "being helpful" move away might be saying yes to driving a friend to the airport in the middle of your workday because you're afraid they will be angry with you if you say no, and you don't want to feel guilty. What looks like the same value is in service of two different things. True values represent moves toward what matters, not moves away from discomfort. Sometimes it helps me to think of a move toward as feeling pulled or called to something, rather than being pushed or shoved from behind.

Values Are Not...

In addition to being freely chosen, ongoing, and moves toward something, values are also *not* limited, emotions, or about feeling better.

Values are not limited. You get to choose from all the options, all the time, irrespective of your history or circumstances.[5] For example, you may find yourself saying, "I used to value romantic relationships until I got burned, and now they don't matter to me anymore, because I just can't deal." Or "I thought I valued career advancement, but it's just not going to happen for me, so what's the point of valuing it?" A person may choose to not prioritize taking action in a given domain at a certain time. But with values, we are talking about what you would choose to make important, what would result in a meaning-filled life, if you lived a life where you were totally free to choose without limit. When I say values are not limited, I'm saying there is no "but I can't choose that because" stipulation when it comes to valuing. Choosing actions and qualities of actions that will bring greater meaning or vitality is 100 percent available to you, 100 percent of the time. Barriers in the form of thoughts and feelings will arise, to be sure. And sometimes there will be barriers to what we can actually do in the world. But the values themselves are not limited. We will talk in great depth about how to overcome the barriers in later chapters.

Values are not emotions. As much as we'd like to believe we can control how we feel, we simply cannot. In fact, it is often the case that the more we try to limit or enhance a feeling, the more of the opposite we get.[6] We will talk much more about this in chapter 9, but it matters here because values must be qualities we can choose. We don't choose how we feel. Therefore, feeling states cannot be values. For example, we can't value being calm, but we can value acting respectfully even when we feel angry.

Values are not about feeling better. When I teach folks about building psychological flexibility, they often say, "Great! If I just live my values, then I'll finally get rid of this self-doubt and anxiety!" Sorry to be the bearer of bad news, but this isn't how it works. Why? Because pursuing what deeply matters is high stakes and can be anxiety inducing. If you are going to boldly go after the new job or share your creative work with others, you will undoubtedly feel more vulnerable. You care about the outcomes, so you worry about performing well. This is exactly where imposterism arises. But that emotional pain is often a signal that you are exactly where you are meant to be. In fact, you can look to your discomfort to better understand what matters to you most, and you can use what matters to you most (your "why") to guide your way forward even when you feel uncomfortable. Comfort has a cost, and discomfort offers gifts. The payoff of learning to flexibly be present with pain is that we can live freely, pursuing paths of opportunity, meaning, vitality, and fulfillment.

When Janina, whom you met in chapter 2, was a doctoral student in my clinical consultation course, she was moved by a discussion our group had about values. Janina knew that in addition to being her professor, I ran an outpatient practice that specialized in providing evidence-based treatment for people struggling with anxiety disorders. Seeing an opportunity to learn about providing these therapies beyond the classroom, Janina had the idea to seek employment at my clinic. The moment it occurred to her, she felt like an imposter. She said to herself, *There's no way she'll actually give me a job. I'm no one. I have no experience. And she's the Jill Stoddard.*

(That last part makes *me* feel like the imposter.) Despite feeling 100 percent certain I'd turn her down and experiencing intense physical panic, self-doubt, and worry about the possibility I might judge her, she decided to go for it. Based on our discussion in class, she told herself, *If I don't do it, I'll regret not even trying.* Janina decided to move toward her values rather than away from her discomfort.

You may remember from chapter 2 that Janina works for me. In fact, we just celebrated our ten-year "workiversary." But the day she asked for a job, I did indeed turn her down. Janina's worst fear came true. And despite the emotional pain this rejection caused, she felt empowered that she chose to embody courage in service of boldly pursuing a meaningful opportunity. A few days after declining to hire Janina, I realized I would be crazy not to create a position for this bright, enthusiastic, courageous go-getter. I followed my values too. In the end, we both won. When I asked Janina if it still would have been worth the ask even if I hadn't changed my mind, she said, "One hundred percent!" When you're choosing values, there's often a feeling—maybe it's a gut feeling or an instinct or wisdom or knowing—that grounded, felt sense of *Yeah, this is right; I should do more of this* that's present even when the outcome you desire doesn't occur. This was definitely the case for Janina and me.

Write Your Epitaph

One of my favorite ways to start thinking about values is by writing an epitaph.[7] I know it sounds morbid, but stick with me here; then we'll play with it in a more still-alive-and-kicking sort of way. An epitaph is a brief inscription, typically engraved on a headstone or monument, in memory of a deceased person. If you were to write yours, what would you want it to say about the way you chose to live?

Would you want your epitaph to say something like the following?

"Here lies **[your name]**. They were skilled at playing it safe to avoid rejection, failure, and imposterism."

"Here lies **[your name]**. They kept all thoughts, feelings, and opinions to themselves to avoid being judged or rejected."

"Here lies **[your name]**. They relentlessly pursued achievements in an effort to feel legitimate, at the cost of missing out on life outside of work."

"Here lies **[your name]**. They avoided challenges for fear of being revealed as a fraud."

Or would you want it to read something more like one of these?

"Here lies **[your name]**. They were skilled at being vulnerable and choosing to risk rejection and failure in service of living boldly and pursuing meaningful opportunities."

"Here lies **[your name]**. They expressed thoughts, feelings, and ideas openly at the risk of being judged, in service of being their authentic self."

"Here lies **[your name]**. They went after opportunities that lit them up while making time for important activities and people outside work."

"Here lies **[your name]**. They embraced challenges despite feeling fear, uncertainty, and self-doubt."

> **Write your own epitaph:**
> Here lies _____.
> They _____
> _____.

When I recently presented the epitaph exercise to a client, her mind didn't generate words; it produced the image of a disco ball. "What does a disco ball represent for you?" I asked. She described an object that was composed of many small imperfect pieces that when put together sparkled and shined. She said a disco ball represented fun, created an approachable energy, and reflected light back to the world. This was exactly how she wanted to be. She wanted to accept her small flaws and focus on what she had to offer as a whole human. She wanted to be a person who reflected other people's light back to them. And she wanted to be fun and approachable. So many values! So if you struggle with the words, consider a symbolic object instead.

Write Your Values-Based Tagline

Not into death-based epitaphs? Let's try creating a values-based tagline instead. Taglines are meant to represent the values and mission of a brand. Here are a few particularly famous ones:

Disneyland: The happiest place on earth.
Nike: Just do it.
Allstate: You're in good hands.
Mastercard: There are some things money can't buy. For everything else, there's Mastercard.

M&M's: Melts in your mouth, not in your hands.

L'Oréal: Because you're worth it.

The most effective taglines are those that are memorable, meaningful (i.e., communicate the benefit), and upbeat or optimistic. So let's develop a few of our own in a similar fashion. Here are some of mine, followed by the values I'm trying to capture:

Jill: Work hard. Play harder. (Industriousness, playfulness, fun, humor.)

Jill: What you see is what you get. (Authenticity.)

Jill: Perfectly imperfect woman in progress. (Acceptance, growth.)

Jill: Live, laugh, love, flex, write. (Presence, humor, love, psychological flexibility, creativity.)

Now you give it a go. Brainstorm a couple of fun taglines, and jot down the qualities they are meant to express. You're always welcome to borrow from mine if they fit for you too!

[Your Name]: _____

(_____)

[Your Name]: _____

(_____)

CHOOSE OR LOSE

We tend to think about decisions as the big things: where to go to college, whether to accept a job offer, when to break off a relationship. Indeed, these are important decisions. But choice abounds in the small moments too. Every moment of every day is a moment we get to choose. What time to get up, what to wear, what to eat, when to leave, where to go, what to do. Do I exercise or hit the snooze button? Do I choose eggs and fruit or doughnuts? Do I look up and smile at my partner or keep my head buried in my phone? Do I drive nine inches from the bumper in front of me, aggressively gripping the steering wheel, cursing out slow drivers in the left lane, or give the car some space and get over myself?

You might be interpreting each of these examples as "good" choices versus "bad." Notice whether your mind judged staying in bed or eating doughnuts—or judged me for judging. In reality, I offered no labels. Choices are neither right nor wrong, good nor bad. They are in service of something: moving toward values or moving away from discomfort. In most of the examples above, the choice could be either of these. Exercise might be a move toward in any number of values-based scenarios: you care about your health; you care about modeling movement for your children; you care about exercising your dog. But pressing snooze can be a move toward too: you were up late caring for a loved one and want to let your body sleep; you're recovering from an illness; you want to practice self-care by snuggling with your kitty under the warm blankets. Exercise can also be a move away: you're unwilling to feel anxiety, so you try to exercise it away even if it means being late for work; you are trying to burn every calorie you consumed the day before to avoid feeling (misplaced) guilt. You may choose to keep your head buried in your phone rather than look up to smile at your partner if you're on a video call with your grandmother. You may even choose to tailgate a slow car in front of you as a way to communicate nonverbally—"Please move over!"—if you're trying to get to the hospital in time to see your child born or before a loved one passes.

The point here is that values are all about making deliberate decisions across different contexts: what you would choose to make important in this present situation if you were doing so in a conscious, thoughtful, unlimited way. Too often we hit the snooze button, eat the doughnut, or drive like a jerk all on autopilot—there is no true choosing happening in the moment. We talked about mindfulness creating a space in which we can make more-deliberate decisions. Psychological flexibility means making a ruthless commitment to choosing our actions based on values, not acting on autopilot to escape pain or in response to unhelpful or urgent thoughts.

Context Matters

Does this mean if you choose exercise over the snooze button today, you are locked into that being your values-based choice forever? Absolutely not. Context matters. The only thing I want you to do forever is consistently ask yourself *What is this in service of?* each time you are faced with a choice. Today's get-up-and-go exercise in service of fitness may be tomorrow's snooze button in service of recovery. Just beware you're not rationalizing and calling it values if it's really avoidance! Remember, certain language (like rationalizations, assumptions, predictions, judgments) can lead to psychological inflexibility. Our choices have to be honest, and this isn't always easy. Avoidance can be clever if we're not approaching choices with our eyes wide open.

I asked my friend Jenna LeJeune, one of the authors of *Values in Therapy*, whether she has any tricks for spotting whether a choice is values based or avoidance in disguise.[8] She said she sometimes looks to her emotional response following a choice she has made. If her predominant reaction is "Phew!" and she feels a sense of relief, this is often a signal she chose an avoidance move. If she feels more alive or notices a sense of vitality, meaning, or pride, this is typically a sign she has chosen a values-based move.

I worked with a client who struggled with emotion regulation in interpersonal relationships. She had a history of abandonment by her father, who remarried and prioritized his second family over her in an extreme way. She was understandably sensitive to perceived rejection as a result. What she wanted was a life in which she felt free to love openly and authentically, amid vulnerability and fear of being hurt. She no longer wanted to shut down or defend herself at the expense of closeness. During our work together, she bravely cultivated a close, healthy relationship with a new boyfriend by centering her values. While their relationship wasn't perfect, they were able to communicate effectively and resolve conflicts as a team. They created a psychologically safe space for one another. Five years later, they are still going strong.

Ideally, my client would have loved to embody openness, lovingness, and authenticity with her father and stepfamily too. However, each time she attempted to do so, they rejected or abandoned her all over again. In this context, my client had to rethink her values. She chose to prioritize safety, self-respect, and self-care, which meant choosing boundaries over openness. You might have a similar family situation, or perhaps you have a boss or work administration that sees vulnerability as weakness and weaponizes it against the staff. If you are a woman, it may be unsafe to express emotion in contexts where you will be labeled "hysterical" or "unstable." If you are Black, it may be unsafe to express anger where you will be labeled an "angry Black man/woman." Our values don't necessarily *change*, but context matters when it comes to choosing which ones to prioritize.

Funerals and the Me You Want to Model

There are a number of different ways to get clear on our values. My podcast cohosts, Debbie Sorensen and Yael Schonbrun, recently shared their personal favorite strategies in an episode on values during times of transition.[9] Debbie, author of *ACT for Burnout: Recharge, Reconnect, and Transform Burnout with Acceptance and Commitment Therapy*, shared that she loves to use a funeral exercise for herself, her clients, and even her husband.[10] She described walking her husband through the exercise, guiding him to envision a crowded funeral where his loved ones took turns talking about him and the way he had chosen to live his life. Prior to the exercise, Debbie and her husband had been on the fence about whether to have children. Envisioning his funeral provided her husband with crystal clarity that he wanted his life to include fatherhood (and luckily, Debbie was on board!).

Yes, we are back to death. Being faced with mortality is a powerful reminder that time is promised to no one, and a life well lived is one that is deliberately chosen. Imagine you have lived life well by choosing values. What would your loved ones say at your funeral?

YOUR FUNERAL

You've lived your best life, choosing values as your guide. What might your loved ones say about you and the life you have lived?

_____

_____

_____

_____

_____

If you want to take it further, now consider what the same people would say if your funeral occurred today. What might they say about how you currently handle imposterism or self-doubt? About the choices you make when you feel anxious or insecure? How is this different from what you imagined above? It may be painful to encounter discrepancies here, but this can also be a launching-off point for how you might start making new choices.

_____

_____

_____

_____

My other cohost, Yael Schonbrun, author of _Work, Parent, Thrive: 12 Science-Backed Strategies to Ditch Guilt, Manage Overwhelm, and Grow Connection (When Everything Feels Like Too Much)_, chooses her values by considering what she wants to model to her three young sons. She shared with Debbie and me that she wants her boys to see a human who is imperfect but tries hard, who has feelings and manages them, who finds balance between professional ambition and being home loving on her kids, and who wants to be of service but wants to chill out sometimes too. When you think about the Me you most deeply desire to be, what does that look like? What do you want the most important people in your life to see in and from you?

THE ME YOU WANT TO MODEL

When you look into the eyes of your most beloved people (or animals) or you look into your own eyes in the mirror, who do you want to see? If a video camera were recording your every move, to be played back to you or to a person who looks up to you, what kinds of choices would you hope to see? Who is the Me you most deeply desire to model and be?

_____

_____

_____

_____

_____

WWJ(ill)D?

When a client of mine came to our therapy session beaming with pride about the values-based choices she had made during the previous week, my heart sang. "What's your secret? How were you able to make those choices?" I asked. "Easy," she said. "For every choice, I just thought, *WWJD?*" My brain went into hyperdrive: *What would Jesus do? Oh my gosh, how did I not know she was religious?*

I'm the worst therapist ever. I can't believe her faith is this important to her and I had no idea. Until she rescued me. She said, "You know, *What would Jill do?*" My client went on to explain that she carried an imaginary Jill on her shoulder, and each time she was faced with a choice, she thought about our sessions and what I would encourage her to do. I loved this so much! Not because I have an over-sized ego and think I'm a regular Jesus, but because she came up with a helpful strategy to center her values.

I adopted the strategy myself and have since taught it to countless clients and workshop attendees. Anyone who knows me knows I'm a little obsessed with Oprah Winfrey, so my WWJD is WWOD: What would Oprah do? I look up to Oprah because she has endured poverty, abuse, racism, sexism, and body shaming and has never let it stop her from being herself and pursuing what matters to her. Though I don't know Oprah personally, she seems to use her money and power to make a positive impact on the world. So when I'm faced with a tough choice, I think, *WWOD?* Consider for yourself who your J or O would be, and plug them in: WW_D?

For those of you who might struggle to model yourself so easily after someone you look up to, you can also try WW_S: what would [your person] say—sometimes a pep talk from someone you admire can go a long way.

Both WWOD and WWOS helped me make an important career decision. Toward the end of 2020 I had the opportunity to give a TEDx talk. For me, it was a dream come true. But I had gained a lot of weight during the pandemic, and as I've already shared, my size has always been a raw spot. I dreaded memorializing myself on YouTube. I felt like a fraud, because *who am I to give anyone advice when I can't even get my own issues under control?* In that moment, I asked myself, *What would Oprah do?* I knew

Oprah would do the talk. She has battled her weight quite publicly but never let it stop her. I also asked myself, *What would Oprah say?* I imagined her saying, "Jill, you are so much more than your body. You have a mission and a message to share. If you might help just one person by sharing that message, you have to get out there and do it. The size of your body is irrelevant." And so I did the talk. If I'm being honest, it's hard for me to watch. But I don't for one single second regret doing the talk. I'm really proud that I let my values make that choice, not my lifelong feelings about my body.

WHAT WOULD YOUR GUIDE DO/SAY?

Who is your WW_D or WW_S? Choose a person you know (relative, teacher, coach, friend) or a person you feel like you know (celebrity, fictional character). If you felt like an imposter or had other self-defeating thoughts or difficult feelings that threatened to get in your way, what would your person do or say that reflects your values?

Name: _____

Action/Message: _____

Name: _____

Action/Message: _____

Name: _____

Action/Message: _____

Values are what you choose to make important in each present moment. They are how you are living when you are living a meaningful life. They are actions and qualities of actions. As such, they are about choice and process, not about outcome. In fact, learning to hold outcomes lightly is a critical piece of the psychological flexibility puzzle.

The Recap: What to Know
- Values can be broken down into three tiers: (1) domains, (2) goals/actions, and (3) qualities.
- Values are personal, freely chosen, ongoing, and moves toward something.
- Values are not limited, not emotions, and not in service of feeling better.
- The values you choose to prioritize may vary depending on context.
- Conscious, deliberate choice is key.

The Work: What to Do
- Complete a values cone with domain, actions, and qualities.
- Write a values-based epitaph and/or tagline.
- Imagine your funeral: What would you hope your loved ones would say about how you chose to live your life?
- Consider the Me you most deeply desire to model and be.
- Choose a guide you admire, and consider what they would do or say if faced with a similar choice (WW_D, WW_S).

Chapter 6

Holding Outcomes Lightly

The summit is what drives us, but the climb itself is what matters.
—Conrad Anker

As a kid, Marshall Mathers was an aspiring comic book artist who was drawn to storytelling. Living in poverty, the son of a single mother, he dropped out of high school and worked several jobs to help pay the bills. When his uncle gifted him the soundtrack to the movie *Breakin'*, Marshall discovered a new format for telling stories: rap music. He began performing in freestyle rap battles and open-mic contests during his limited free time. Soon, the artist known as Eminem was born. Eminem struggled to fit in as the only white rapper in the Detroit hip-hop scene. His first album was a commercial failure, and critics suggested he change music genres from hip-hop to rock and roll. Eminem's early struggles to be accepted in the hip-hop music scene, along with poverty, substance use, and depression, threatened to undermine his creative and professional journey. But instead of giving up when he didn't achieve the outcomes he desired, Eminem doubled down on his music. He wrote controversial lyrics that allowed him to express his emotions around serious themes like drugs, violence, poverty, and mental illness. At the age of twenty-five, nine years after beginning his rap journey, Eminem won second place in the Rap Olympics. He was discovered by record company executive Jimmy Iovine and music producer Dr. Dre. Although Dr. Dre was criticized by his associates for hiring a white rapper, Dre and Iovine went on to catapult Eminem to hip-hop stardom, making him one of the best-selling music artists of all time and earning the respect of his peers along the way.

On November 5, 2022, Eminem was inducted into the Rock & Roll Hall of Fame. Dr. Dre introduced him, saying, "Turns out this unassuming white guy with blue eyes from Detroit went from being repeatedly turned down to turning everything we thought we knew about hip-hop on its head while forcing us to confront our own biases, growing not only the genre, but all of us right along with it."

Perhaps Eminem seems like an unusual example to use. He has certainly generated his fair share of controversy. But he's an excellent example of someone who persevered through failure to achieve his goals in a space where he likely felt (and was explicitly told) he didn't belong—where I imagine an imposter story likely resided (and in his speech at the Rock & Roll Hall of Fame induction he said, "I'm probably not supposed to actually be here tonight"). Once destitute and unknown, he skyrocketed to fortune and fame. But first Eminem struggled for nearly a decade. What is the difference between those who keep going after years of failure and you-don't-belong-here messages and those who quit? I don't know Eminem personally, but I'd bet he had a clear "why" that transcended goal achievement during that time. He is an artist and a creator who loves to perform and has a message to share. I'm guessing if Marshall Mathers never became the Grammy-, Emmy-, and Oscar-winning Eminem, he'd still be writing rhymes and competing in rap battles. Would he still desire to make it? Would selling records and earning the respect of his peers still be his goal? Most certainly. *And* he'd likely keep going even if he never landed on those outcomes.

REDEFINING SUCCESS

Would we still consider Marshall Mathers a success if he never became the famous Eminem? In many cultures, success is defined almost exclusively by goal achievement. Think about a handful of people whom you would consider successful. Now consider what makes them successful in your eyes. Most likely, these are people who have achieved specific, lofty goals. The problem with this outlook on success, though, is its flip side: that not achieving a specified goal makes a person a failure. Yikes.

I'm going to go out on a limb here and suggest that we have this all wrong. Because here's the thing: goals are often outcomes that are largely out of our control. When I think about my biggest goal for this book, it would be to land on the *New York Times* bestseller list. So if the book doesn't make it onto the list, does that make me a failure? If I do everything perfectly, work my butt off, and write a great book, is it still possible I won't land on the *New York Times* bestseller list? *Absolutely.* Fewer than five hundred books make it onto the preeminent list each year—that's less than 1 percent of published books. Does that mean the other 99.5 percent of books are garbage and so are their authors? Does it mean we're not real writers? Of course not. There are a lot of choices I can make and steps or actions I can take to make my book more likely to be a *New York Times* bestseller, but whether it happens is not really up to me.

An overfocus on goal achievement as our only metric of success is highly problematic.

Consider this for yourself. If I asked you to identify two to three goals, personal or professional, what would they be?

1. _____
2. _____
3. _____

Looking those goals over, are you 100 percent in charge of completing them? Let me give you some examples of big goals that are outcomes that aren't entirely up to you:

1. Get a promotion or job
2. Get ten thousand followers, a thousand likes, a million downloads, five thousand subscribers
3. Get an agent, get published, get a part
4. Find a partner or spouse
5. Make a million dollars
6. Find and buy the perfect house
7. Hold a political office or become an organizational board member or officer
8. Get straight As
9. Get accepted to a specific sorority, fraternity, college, graduate school
10. Win a Nobel Prize, a Pulitzer, or any other award

Do you see it? There are many steps you can take to make goals like this more *likely*, but many factors outside of you determine whether these outcomes are actually realized. Social media algorithms may not work in your favor; you may live in a district that leans in the opposite direction of your political messaging; you may lack resources that those in competition with you have access to. The potential external obstacles are many. If you encounter these obstacles and run for a political or organizational seat and lose the election, are you done? Or do you rap on like Eminem? What if, instead of specifying *outcomes*, your goals pointed to *actions* and *qualities of actions* in domains that matter to you? Sound familiar? Unlike outcomes, *these* are what we have the ability to influence. We can pick any of the ten goals listed above and create a values cone. Here's an example to replace goal number seven: *Hold a political office or become an organizational board member or officer.*

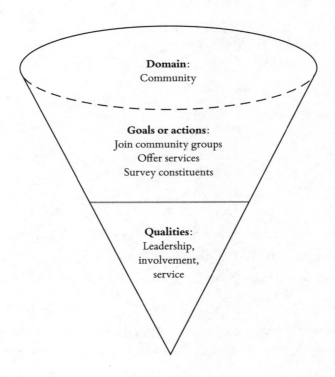

In this example, if a person loses an election, they can keep choosing valued actions and qualities of actions in domains that matter, like continuing to contribute to the community in philanthropic ways. We control actions and qualities; we don't control outcomes.

Consider a goal of your own that is structured around an uncontrollable outcome. Can you rework it to fit into a values cone?

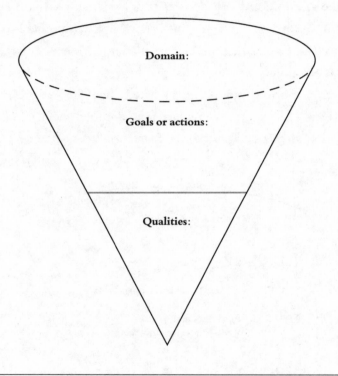

Domain:

Goals or actions:

Qualities:

We need to redefine success not as the achievement of outcome-oriented goals, but as the consistent choosing of valued actions irrespective of outcome.

In other words, you can fail to get the job, the promotion, the followers, the agent, the money, or the grades and still choose to show up and give it your all because you're clear on your why. This doesn't mean you won't *feel* disappointed, discouraged, dejected, or any other number of sad adjectives that begin with the letter *D*. But keeping your why close by and choosing to show up as the kind of person you want to be—maybe one who persists through failure, who chooses courage and willingness, who engages in lifelong learning and skill building—brings a greater sense of meaning and vitality to life. It also makes desired outcomes more likely. One surefire way to never reach your dreams is to give up on them.

Build Identity and Make Up Your Mind

In his best-selling book, *Atomic Habits*, James Clear differentiates between outcomes, processes (the actions we take), and identity. He recommends building identity-based habits rather than outcome-based habits, which means focusing on who we wish to become, rather than what we hope to achieve (sound familiar?). So instead of turning down a drink because you're "trying to cut down," you turn down the drink because you're "not a drinker." Clear states, "The ultimate form of intrinsic motivation is when a habit becomes part of your identity.... The more pride you have in a particular aspect of your identity, the more motivated you will be to maintain the habits associated with it."[1] Eminem is a rapper. I am a writer. Who are you?

I spoke to Eve Rodsky, best-selling author of *Fair Play: A Game-Changing Solution for When You Have Too Much to Do (and More Life to Live)* and *Find Your Unicorn Space: Reclaim Your Creative Life in a Too-Busy World*. She told me the best way she has found to move forward in the face of uncertainty and imposterism is to remember the Rosa Parks quote "When one's mind is made up, this diminishes fear." Eve combines preparation, science, data, and her own personal experiences to make up her mind. Instead of focusing strictly on a desired outcome, for Eve, making up her mind makes it "easier to do that thing and know it has value even if everyone tells you it doesn't." It helps her "bust through the fear of being rejected."

When Goal Achievement Backfires

In much the same way failing to achieve an outcome-oriented goal can stop you in your tracks, so can accomplishing the stated goal. Consider what might happen when you do get the job or win the election. Being clear on your why (or your identity or having your mind made up) still needs to be front and center so that checking the goal off your to-do list doesn't signal you're finished. In her book *Get It Done*, Ayelet Fishbach cites research that finds individuals who achieve their goals limit their actions until a new target is in sight. For example, a runner who sets a goal to complete 26.2 miles will relax her running regimen until another marathon is on the horizon, even if that horizon is a year or more away.[2] This seems counterproductive if your reasons for running are related to values that deeply matter to you—perhaps things like fitness, challenge, presence, persistence, or skillfulness—rather than just completing an outcome-oriented goal every once in a while.

Several years ago, I set a goal to run my first 5K. I completed a Couch to 5K training program and ran the race on Mother's Day. Having a stated goal motivated me to train. But my first 5K was also my last. I had failed to connect the goal to my values. It wasn't until I identified how deeply important modeling healthy living to my kids was to me—that was my value—that I became a consistent exerciser. Recently, a new doctor referred to me as "an athlete," and I burst out laughing. I hadn't quite gotten to that identity piece yet. "I'm a writer" took about twelve years. But I'm trying "I'm an athlete" on for size in service of building habits that last longer than those strictly dictated by outcome-based goals.

What happens when achieving your goal triggers imposterism? That oh-my-god-I-can't-believe-I-got-the-job-who-am-I-I'm-nobody-I'm-a-fraud narrative that threatens to scare you into giving up or burning yourself out by overachieving to prove yourself. If you hold the outcomes more lightly and keep your why close by, you can keep choosing the actions and qualities of actions that represent the Me you most want to be.

<hr>

Hold Outcomes Lightly[3]

Right now, find something you can hold in your hand: a pen, pencil, or tube of lip balm. Think about an outcome-based goal you've been working toward. Consider all the energy, attention, and effort you've been putting into achieving this goal. Now squeeze the object as hard as would represent all that effort you've been putting into accomplishing your goal, and notice how it feels. Where would you rate the strength of your grip on a scale of zero to ten? Now release the object about 50 percent (so if you were at an eight, hold it at a four), and notice how it feels. Now hold the object as lightly as you can without dropping it, and notice how it feels. What is the one thing that hasn't changed? You are still holding the object. So how might you continue to move forward with actions that make achieving your goal more likely, centering qualities you value, while holding the outcome more lightly?

POINTS OF POSSIBILITY

When I was in graduate school, an administrator at the anxiety clinic where I trained chastised me for laughing too loudly. I was in my back office, where clients couldn't hear, but she wanted me to pipe down nonetheless, so I did. A few days later, that same administrator chastised me for not smiling enough. I apologized and tried to smile more but without laughing too loudly. I wanted to fit in, to be seen as acceptable. Especially as a way to prevent being outed for the fraud I feared I was. The program culture was such that you got in trouble for calling in sick, and you also got in trouble for showing up sick. It felt impossible to win. I remember thinking, *Maybe if I got struck by a car, not so hard as to cause permanent damage but enough to make a hospital stay legitimate, I could get a break without getting in trouble.*

As toxic as that was, in a way, I now see it as a gift. It made me realize that in the same way we can't control outcomes, we also can't control other people—their thoughts, feelings, expectations, or actions. The only thing we can control is how we choose to move our bodies and use our voices in each present moment. And each present moment is a point of possibility (POP). What might be possible— how might your life *pop*—if you chose values over comfort?

When I stopped laughing and started smiling, I wasn't really choosing. I was being who I thought this administrator wanted me to be, in an attempt to control an outcome—to make her like me and win her approval.

It was an old pattern devoid of new possibilities. If I had a do-over today, I would consider what might be possible if I chose to center my values. If I asked myself, *Who is the Me I most deeply wish to be at this POP? What would I choose to make important in this context that would make my life* pop? the answers would revolve around authenticity. I would choose to smile when I felt joy or pleasure or wanted to connect with another person. I would not smile if I felt sadness, fear, or any other emotion that was inconsistent with smiling for me. I would laugh when amused. Would I have spoken up for myself? I'd like to think I would today, but I probably would not have back then, even if considering my values. This was a context with a clear power differential, and historically, standing up to those who evaluated us didn't go well. But I wouldn't be shutting up on autopilot out of fear. I would be *choosing* to keep my comments to myself as a way to embody my values of safety and self-preservation.

Values don't tend to change dramatically over time. However, as we talked about in chapter 5, context matters. The qualities you choose to embody in one setting or interpersonal situation may differ from the ones you choose in the next. You may most often choose to be open and authentic in interpersonal relationships *and* choose to have strict boundaries in relationships where vulnerability has repeatedly been weaponized against you. What is important is that you are choosing thoughtfully and deliberately, rather than applying a set of values in a rigid, rule-governed way.

Consulting a Values Expert

The process of values identification is one of ongoing exploration and discovery. At this point, you may have a greater sense of clarity around how you want to show up as you navigate your world when it comes to certain actions, qualities, and contexts, while holding outcomes lightly. You also may be feeling a little confused about how to go about putting some of your values into practice.

Reading and writing—what we've been doing so far—are a great start. But valued living is about doing. If you're not sure what "doing" love, presence, authenticity, bravery, or any other value would look like, you can do what you do when you see a dentist for a toothache or an accountant for your taxes: consult an expert.[4]

Choose a value you'd like to prioritize putting into practice. Now think of someone you know who does a masterful job living out that value. Ask to interview them. What are you most curious about here? Prepare questions that will help you explore what this value might look like as behavior so you might discover ideas for workable actions of your own.

Here's an example of the value of courage. You might approach this person by saying something like "I really admire the way you take on challenges. I've noticed you freely share your opinion and make bold moves in your career. To me, this exemplifies courage, which is a value I hold dear and would like to embody more. Would you be willing to answer some questions about how you've been able to do this so well?"

You might ask questions like the following:

1. What does living courageously mean to you?
2. How have you put courage into practice?
3. Have you always lived courageously? If not, what made you center this value, and how were you able to make the change?
4. What have you noticed about yourself, your relationships, or your career since you started living courageously? Have things changed for you?
5. How do you think living courageously impacts others?
6. What gets in the way of your choosing to act courageously? What helps you when you get stuck?

If a formal interview isn't your style, you can tap into the same information over coffee or lunch in a more informal conversation. Either way, once you complete your interview or conversation, spend some time reflecting on what you learned. Consider why you chose this particular person and how you're feeling about the interaction. What did you learn that might help you put your chosen value into practice? Knowing things might get in the way, did the wisdom and experience of your chosen person encourage you to move forward nonetheless? Consider how your life might feel different if you were to commit to embodying this value.

The Four Ps

Each present moment is a POP—an opportunity to let go of outcomes (or at least hold them more lightly) and center values in deciding what to say or how to act. You can break down each POP into the Four *P*s:

Pause: Take a beat, and recognize you are at a POP—here it is! Ask yourself, *What do I want this moment to be in service of: moving toward my values or away from discomfort?* Often choices in service of comfort end up being choices away from values (though not always).

Pick: Now choose—what are the values you wish to live out in this context? Who is the Me you want to be in this moment?

Persist or Pivot: Based on the values you picked, do you wish to persist with your current behavior or pivot to a new action and/or quality of action that is more values congruent?

All we have is this one present moment. The past is gone, and the future has yet to happen. Even as you've been reading this chapter, you've encountered several present moments where you've gotten to choose the Me you want to be: Do you skim, daydream, and skip the exercises? Or do you give your full attention and effort? There is no right or wrong, just pausing, picking, and persisting or pivoting in each moment, based on values.

Notice the word *moment*. Right there in the middle is the word *me*. Me in the middle of this mo*me*nt. When you are in present moments—POPs—you can picture this word and ask yourself, *Who is the Me I most want to be in this one moment?*

MOM**E**NT

It's perfectly fine to have future-oriented goals you want to work toward. I'm not suggesting you ditch those altogether. But I want you to connect them to your values—to show up to each present moment consciously as you pursue your goals, holding outcomes lightly and choosing actions and qualities of actions centered around the Me you want to be. Values create intrinsic motivation wherein the pursuit of an activity feels like an end in itself—it's something we *want* to do rather than something we *have* to do. When the actions we take in service of goal achievement are more intrinsically motivating, we are more likely to persist (even if we don't get the outcome we desire).[5] It's not always easy. Often choosing what matters feels more vulnerable and has higher stakes. Craving the comfort zone can get in the way. So can listening to our harsh inner critic.

The Recap: What to Know

- Being overly focused on goal achievement as our only metric of success is problematic, especially when goals are outcomes.
- Outcomes are often out of our control.
- Actions (how we move our bodies and use our voices) are in our control.
- We can redefine success as the consistent choosing of valued actions irrespective of outcome.
- Each present moment is a point of possibility (POP). Decide how to proceed by using the Four *P*s: pause, pick, and persist or pivot.

The Work: What to Do

- Rework your outcome-oriented goals by using the values cone.
- Interview a person who successfully lives by a value you wish to embody.
- At POPs, use the Four *P*s to center values.
- Choose the Me you want to be in each moment.

Chapter 7

The Harsh Inner Critic

*You think, "Why would anyone want to see me again in a movie?
And I don't know how to act anyway, so why am I doing this?"*
—Meryl Streep, most Oscar-nominated actor of all time

When my second book, *Be Mighty*, came out, I was fortunate to land a number of guest appearances on podcasts and other media outlets. One of these was my second appearance on my favorite podcast, *Psychologists Off the Clock* (*POTC*). In preparing for the book launch, it became clear that while being a podcast guest could be a helpful tool for getting the word out, becoming a podcast host had even more potential. Podcasting was quickly becoming an increasingly popular method for authors and other professionals to build platforms for expanding their market reach. Outside of being an interviewed guest and a listener, I knew nothing about podcasting. So shortly after my second *POTC* interview, I reached out to the cohosts to get their advice on possibly starting my own podcast. Instead, they invited me to be a permanent cohost of *POTC*. I couldn't believe it. And to no one's surprise, my inner critic and imposter voice couldn't believe it either. *Oh jeez, I totally fooled them. I have no idea what I'm doing. I'm a fan, not a host. At best, I'm a guest, but a host? I'll sound ridiculous. They'll all figure out I am incompetent and have no business talking to smart, famous people about their work!* My mind was on overdrive. But was it trying to sabotage me, or was something else going on?

CONFRONTING THE INNER CRITIC

Our minds are master critics. But unlike Siskel and Ebert, who at least sometimes gave two thumbs up to movies, our inner critics are prone to a negativity bias, finding reasons to give two thumbs down to any number of situations with painful frequency. While this seems unnecessarily cruel, having an inner critic is designed to be helpful. Remember, early humans who hunted, gathered, and migrated together had a survival advantage. We didn't have scales or claws to protect us; we had each other. Ensuring we maintained our status among our people was life or death: *Do I measure up? Do I provide value?* An inner voice that says *I'm not good enough; I don't belong here* is designed to keep us on our toes, to prevent us from becoming complacent and losing our footing in our community. This inner critic appears to be a nearly universal human experience that we inherited through evolution.[1]

Pause right now, and consider a painful thought that gives you trouble—one that has been around for a long time, that is familiar, that feels compelling and true. I'm willing to bet you are not scratching your chin, puzzled, unable to generate such a thought. More likely, you're thinking, *Huh, which one? I have so many!* I've asked this question in many therapy sessions and professional trainings, and I have yet to find someone who doesn't have this critical inner voice. It can feel like that voice is trying to hold us back—and perhaps yours has done just that. But maybe the opposite is true. Maybe our inner critics are trying to protect us or help us in some way.

What if you were to talk to your inner critic and ask, "What is it that you want for me? What are you afraid would happen if you stopped critiquing and criticizing me? What are you trying to do for me?" How might that voice answer? Here are a few examples of things your inner critic might say and how it might be trying to help. Fill in the blank row with your own:

You're not good enough.	I'm trying to help you be better and protect you from failure.
You're out of shape.	I'm trying to keep you healthy and protect you from illness, early death, judgment, and rejection.
You're a fraud.	I'm trying to help you succeed and protect you from humiliation.

Here's the thing—if nearly every human being is walking around with an inner critic, it can't be the case that this is a pathology that can be fixed. I'm sure you would love to shut your inner critic up. I'm betting you've even tried. I know I have. And it has never worked. Notice what happens when you argue with your inner critic. When I attempt to convince myself of all the ways I am good enough or not an imposter, my mind just pipes in with *Yeah, but . . .* and fills in compelling data to prove otherwise. We evolved to live with this inner voice. We wouldn't want to strip a chameleon of its camouflage (even if the chameleon thought it was ugly); perhaps we don't need to silence our inner critics either.

The Thought Suppression Paradox

Research has shown that attempts to change or suppress thoughts often backfire.[2] For example, in one study, subjects were asked to not think about white bears. Not only were their efforts unsuccessful, but they thought about white bears significantly more than did the subjects who were asked to think about white bears.[3]

You can check the science against your own experience. Try this: think of a red balloon, and say "Red balloon" five times. Now try as hard as you can to not think about a red balloon. Take a minute and notice what happens. Now choose any object in the room, and focus on that object as a way to inhibit thinking about the red balloon. Notice what happens. For me, when I focus on my pink lamp, a red balloon keeps floating up behind it to the tune of "99 Red Balloons" by Nena. And now I'm thinking about Pennywise from *It*, all the while feeling frustrated that I can't suppress the balloon thoughts, annoyed to have a song I don't like stuck in my head, and scared of Stephen King's killer clown. What a mess!

Part of the reason thought suppression is ineffective is that each time you check whether you're successfully avoiding a thought (*Is it working? Am I not thinking about the red balloon?*), the act of checking brings that thought to mind.

The Borg, cybernetic aliens from *Star Trek: The Next Generation*, were on to something with their threatening catchphrase, "Resistance is futile," and there's a reason this phrase is so recognizable in pop culture—we all get it, even if we've never seen an entire episode of *Star Trek* in our lives (raises hand, much to her husband's chagrin). What we need is a different way. We need to see critical thoughts, of the imposter variety and beyond, as just thoughts—sounds, syllables, and images—that we can choose to relate to in more or less helpful ways. In other words, our inner critic is not our problem. It is the habitual, psychologically inflexible patterns we've learned in response to that inner voice that keep us stuck.

A client once compared our minds to door-to-door salespeople. These pushy peddlers try to sell us on our thoughts. They use urgency to try to get us to buy what they are selling, and we give in to relieve the sense of urgency and to get the high-pressure salesperson to just shut up and go away. But many times, once the salesperson has gone, we're left wanting to return what we bought, only it's too late. In chapter 8, I will teach you how to forge a new relationship with your inner pushy salesperson, who tries to get you to "buy" your imposter voice and other self-critical thoughts—but first let's dig a little deeper into patterns of thinking and behaving that might be getting in your way. Recognizing these patterns is a critical first step to changing them.

Sticky Thought Patterns

Humans have over six thousand thoughts churning through their minds on any given day,[4] the negative ones grabbing our attention more than others.[5] As we grow up, our thoughts develop as a way to make sense of our experiences.[6] If you were a child who was neglected by your parents, you might develop thoughts like *I'm not important. People who are supposed to care for me can't be trusted.* Thoughts lead to behaviors that protect us at the time they develop. So perhaps you become fiercely self-reliant, ensuring you will be OK even as your parents fail to take care of you. This results in a lower exposure to harm. However, as an adult, you may continue to withhold trust in relationships and not allow yourself to count on others. While this may make you feel safe and in control, ultimately, it will erode your relationships and likely lead to burnout and loneliness. It works...until it doesn't. What's more, when your relationships fail, this will reinforce the belief *I'm not important. People who are supposed to care for me can't be trusted.*

Julie Lythcott-Haims, former Stanford dean and author of four books, including the *New York Times* bestsellers *How to Raise an*

Adult: Break Free of the Overparenting Trap and Prepare Your Kid for Success and *Your Turn: How to Be an Adult*, shared her experience as a Black and biracial twenty-year-old college student living in a fatphobic culture.[7] Julie developed a hacking cough and made an appointment at the student health center. After she waited an inordinate amount of time, a physician finally came in to see her, making no eye contact and greeting her with "Do you realize how much WEIGHT you've gained since you got to Stanford?" He appeared shocked and sounded angry. He shoved papers at her, lectured her, and commanded her to follow a 1,200-calorie diet. He did not ask a single question about her cough. In fact, Julie had to ask him "What about my cough?" to which he dismissively replied, "Oh. We'll give you antibiotics for that." Julie rushed out of the health center, enveloped in shame, and broke down in tears. Incidentally, she was not suffering from a single weight-related health issue.

This experience caused Julie to develop thoughts like *Providers who are supposed to provide care will shame people like me. Doctors can't be trusted to provide safe or adequate care to people like me.* She stopped going to doctors as a way to reduce her exposure to threat. When an acute need arose, she visited urgent care (where, she presumed, they would be less focused on her weight), or she waited to get care until she lost a significant amount of weight. Given her beliefs, this made sense. It "worked" (to give her a sense of protection) until it didn't (she sacrificed care for months, even when suffering in significant ways).

Getting hooked by thoughts and stories led Julie to avoidant behavior that came at the cost of her health-related values. It also created more-problematic outcomes than those her avoidance was designed to protect her from in the first place.

By avoiding doctors, Julie was trying to avoid not only criticism and shame but also the memories of her past painful experience.

But whenever she developed problematic symptoms that indicated she needed to seek medical care, they became a reminder of why she was choosing not to. In other words, she may have been haunted by the original shaming experience *more* when she avoided seeing a doctor (or at least just as much). She also put herself at greater risk by avoiding regular care. When Julie avoided getting care, the absence of a shame experience reinforced the belief *I'm only OK because I avoided the doctor.* Avoiding care was also a sure-fire way to incur criticism from doctors, reinforcing her original beliefs, *Providers who are supposed to provide care will shame people like me. Doctors can't be trusted to provide safe or adequate care to people like me.*

Now, let's look at another example, one that is specific to imposterism.

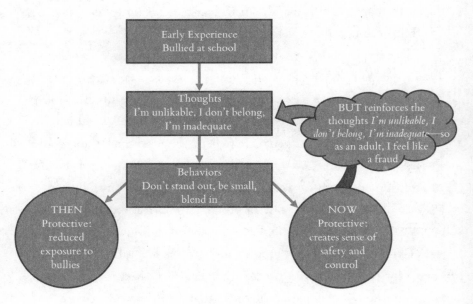

It's easy to get caught up in these patterns. The perception of safety and control is seductive. But at what cost? What thoughts and stories have you developed as a result of your own life experiences, including those related to imposterism and marginaliza-tion? What protective behaviors have emerged as a result? How did they keep you safe then, and how do they feel protective now? *How are they keeping you stuck?* Complete your own cycle below.

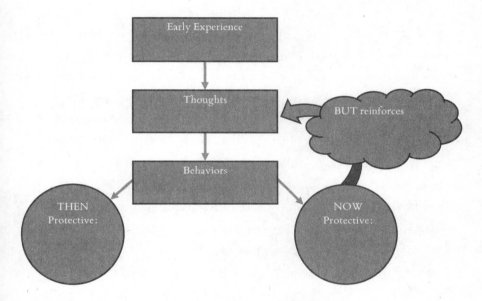

Developing a better understanding of your thought and behav-ior patterns will allow you to become more aware of your deto-nators and bombs—the triggers and automatic reactions that may bring comfort, relief, or a sense of safety, but are not consistent with your values. That awareness is crucial for deactivating the bombs, which we'll talk about in the next chapter.

Julie still feels anxious when she steps on the scale at medical appointments, and she still hears that awful doctor from 1988 in her mind. But she has stopped letting others' opinions about her body impact her right to live well and enjoy her life by accessing the care available to her. She has even taken her experience one step farther by volunteering to serve on the board of the Black

Women's Health Imperative, a leading nonprofit organization that supports the health of Black women and girls. Julie is a shining example of how we can shift old patterns of psychological inflexibility to broader repertoires of values-rich living.

My own pattern is to independence-and-competence my way through things. I had a mom who let me down a lot and whose love was conditional on academic success. So I developed the thought *You can't count on others; you have to do everything well and on your own.* My behavior of juggling All the Things independently and competently helped avoid disappointment and criticism and even contributed to my success. It worked...until it didn't. Eventually, I tried to juggle one too many balls on my own (or more like twenty-seven too many), and they eventually all came crashing down. No one can get through life doing everything on their own forever. Now I notice when I'm struggling to ask for help but really need it. Sometimes when I ask, I end up disappointed. But most times I'm reminded I have amazing people in my life who are happy to support me. Each time I take the risk, my experience reminds me that not everyone is the same as my mom. It also shows me who is more or less likely to be able to meet my needs, which is important information we learn only through experience, not through language (assumptions, predictions, judgments).

You're now about halfway through this book. You hopefully have a better understanding of imposterism, values, and the patterns that are no longer working for you. In the remaining chapters, you will learn to manage the thoughts and feelings that get in the way of valued living, so you are better equipped to choose behaviors that allow you to live full-size. It's time to let go of those not-so-fun-size automatic patterned responses that are no longer serving you.

The thoughts that give us trouble, that are familiar and compelling, don't tend to change much over time, no matter how hard we try. Evolution has hardwired us to focus more on the negative as we try to make sense of the world.[8] But we can recognize the thoughts that lead to unworkable patterns of behavior, and we can choose to respond to them differently. Sometimes listening to your thoughts will be the values-congruent choice; other times it will not. Remember, the number one goal of this book is to build psychological flexibility—this means changing our *relationship* with self-critical imposter thoughts and knowing when it's helpful to listen, when it's not, and what to do instead.

The Recap: What to Know

- Self-critical thoughts, including imposter thoughts, are a normal part of being human.
- Your inner critic is trying to help and protect you.
- Attempts to control or suppress thoughts backfire and give thoughts more power.
- Self-protective behaviors work…until they don't.

The Work: What to Do

In a journal, on your computer, or in the margins, jot down the following:

- How your self-critical thoughts might be trying to help or protect you
- Your patterns of experience, thoughts, and behaviors (as a way to understand what was once helpful but is no longer serving you)

Chapter 8

Choosing When to Listen
(and How Not To)

There will always be critics and naysayers telling you what you cannot do . . . They motivate you to rise above, to challenge yourself, to prove them wrong.

—*José Andrés*

Early in my career as a psychologist, I worked as a therapist for a healthcare organization that valued its researchers more than its clinicians. The clinical staff provided the care for its patients, but the researchers brought in grant money. I felt overworked, underappreciated, and uninspired. Aware of this and wanting to help, a friend alerted me to a faculty position in a local psychology doctoral program. In this role, I'd wear many hats: teacher, researcher, mentor, and clinician. I'd work at the university four days each week and then work in a private practice on the fifth day so students would get the benefit of professors who practiced what they preached. This was not a traditional academic setting. Research was encouraged and small seed-money grants were given to new faculty for start-up labs, but unlike traditional doctoral programs, salaries were hard money (i.e., guaranteed) and not reliant on grants. When I interviewed for the position, three things happened. First, just prior to the start of my job talk (an oral presentation given to the department about my work), the faculty entered the room smiling, chatting, and *hugging* each other in greeting. I had never seen anything like it in traditional academia. Second, my New York Yankees–fan would-be boss told me the only way I wouldn't get an offer was if I was a Red Sox fan. He knew I was from Boston and was already giving me shit for it. I loved him. Third, when a faculty member who knew I was interviewing for another position joked, "Our program is better than theirs," his psychoanalytic colleague, who knew I was a behaviorist, replied, "We don't sink to those primitive defenses here," and she winked at me. I knew all viewpoints would be welcomed there.

Once I got the offer, taking the job should have been a no-brainer, right? I'd get to work in various roles, be valued as a clinician, and work with people who were connected to each other, funny, and accepting. I tried telling that to my mind, but here's what she had to say: *How are you going to mentor students doing research projects when you suck at research? Stats? You* are *going to help students with stats? What a joke. How long do you think you can fake it before you're found out? You'd be lucky to last a semester.*

Complicating matters was the fact that I got my PhD in one of those traditional academic settings. In my program, we were (wrongfully) led to believe that the type of university I was applying to work at (in psychology, it's called a professional school) was subpar. I felt incredibly fortunate for my education—like the faculty took a huge chance giving me one of only twelve spots in my cohort, which I never felt like I deserved. So my mind had a few choice words about that too. *How could you even consider going over to the dark side like this? You will let all your former mentors down and make them regret taking a chance on you. Your reputation will be in the gutter.*

I had a difficult decision to make. I could follow my gut, wisdom, and values, all of which said this would be the perfect job for me. Or I could listen to my inner critic and imposter voice and stay at the hospital job. That may sound like it should have been an easy decision, but with the inner critic and imposter thoughts—thoughts that were trying to protect me from possible failure, humiliation, and rejection—came a lot of fear, uncertainty, and self-doubt. Not running from those feelings and risking that my mind was right, all while leaving a perfectly stable paycheck behind, felt like a huge risk.

Making big decisions that involve change almost always feels risky. There is no way to know what the outcome will be. It makes sense that thoughts and feelings often become obstacles to forward movement.

By this time, I had been learning, teaching, and cultivating psychological flexibility for about eight years. With the tools I used and taught, I buckled down and observed my unhelpful thoughts in a curious but dispassionate way. I recognized the ways they were trying to protect me from making a mistake. I made space for the fear, doubt, and uncertainty. I held the outcomes lightly. And I paid very close attention to my values—the Me I most wanted to be when it came to my career. I didn't want to stay in an uninspiring job simply to avoid the feelings of guilt that might arise if I let my former program director down. I didn't want to pass up an exciting growth opportunity because I felt like a fraud. I loved teaching and had even won awards for it. I wanted to embody that zest again.

At the POP, with zest, courage, willingness, and skill building at the helm (I really did need to brush up on my stats, though not as much as my bullying mind tried to make me believe), I chose to be true to myself and my values, irrespective of my internal experiences: I accepted the position. And I loved it. I even won the outstanding faculty award in my second year. When I finally confessed to the director of my former PhD program that I had gone to the dark side, he was thrilled for me. He had remembered my earlier teaching awards and my skills as a clinician. It turns out I hadn't been fooling anyone into thinking I was a traditional academic type anyway. Thank goodness I didn't let that or any of my other difficult thoughts or feelings make the decision for me.

FORGING A NEW RELATIONSHIP WITH IMPOSTER THOUGHTS

Thoughts and feelings share a bidirectional relationship. If your supervisor requests a meeting and you think, *Oh shit, I'm totally getting fired*, you're likely to feel dread or anxiety (or maybe hope and joy if you hate your job—fingers crossed for a severance package!). If you're feeling anxious and you encounter an ambiguous statement, you are more likely to interpret it as threatening rather than neutral.[1] In other words, thoughts affect how we feel, and feelings affect how we think. Both thoughts and feelings can affect how we act...if we let them.

For the past fifty years, the prevailing psychological theory about thoughts and mental health has suggested that because the way we think impacts the way we feel, we must change our thoughts in order to change how we feel. Research has offered some support for this idea.[2] If you look at your personal experience too, you may see how this *can* be helpful. For example, bring to mind a painfully boring meeting or mandatory HR training you've had to sit through. Consider what went through your mind: *This is useless. What a waste of time. When is this going to be over? Why do they make me sit through this? How much longer are we going to belabor this point?* And so on. How did you feel? Probably bored, annoyed, frustrated, and impatient. It's easy to blame the training, but in reality, situations don't cause feelings. The way we think about them does. Think of it like an equation:

A (antecedent: the trigger)

↓

B (beliefs: the way you think about A)

↓

C (consequence: how you feel as a result)

In some situations, we can add a **D (dispute: a new B, belief)**. And then when we **E (evaluate: determine whether the C, consequence, has changed)**, we see that changing our cognitive perspective has benefit. So if instead of thinking *When is this awful waste-of-time training going to end?* we think something like *This isn't the end of the world; in the grand scheme of things, it's not that much time, and getting pissed off isn't going to make the time pass faster—it will end soon enough*, we may not feel magically happy, but we may feel less bored, annoyed, frustrated, and impatient. We may also be more likely to learn or benefit from the training experience.

The problem arises when we apply this same strategy to thoughts that are less amenable to disputes. We talked in the last chapter about the evolutionary origins of *I'm not good enough* thoughts and the paradoxical impact of thought suppression (don't think of a red balloon). Attempting to just not think about something painful not only doesn't work but can backfire and make those thoughts increase in frequency, intensity, and duration. Likewise, trying to change entrenched thoughts by convincing ourselves they're not true can also backfire.

My friend and colleague Brian is a successful early-career psychologist. He has a doctoral degree, works in a thriving practice, wrote a book, hosts a podcast, sits on and chairs professional committees, volunteers to help others, and is considered an expert in the growing field of psychedelic psychotherapy. He also happens to be a kick-ass guitar player. Here's what happens when Brian tries to change his very old *I'm inadequate* thoughts:

Thoughts	Disputes that Backfire
I'm inadequate.	No you're not! You're doing fantastic: you have a great group of friends and family, you have a great job, and you work really hard!
Yeah, but I think I've just gotten lucky. I don't think I really deserve to be where I am.	How can you say that? You work really hard, volunteer a lot of your time to help others, and are such a caring, loving guy.
I might be caring, but I've wasted so much time goofing off and not applying myself. I had more potential, and I blew it. At my core, I'm a disappointment.	But look at where you are: you have a PhD and a successful job, you're writing a book, you have your own podcast, and you are establishing yourself in your field.
I achieved those things only because they came easy to me. I should have worked harder.	You spent nine years in graduate school and two years in postdoc, sacrificing a regular income to study and learn. You were so disciplined!
Exactly. I should be way farther along than I am now. I'm an embarrassment.	Yeesh, I give up. You suck.

Brian could keep going and going and going here. Or rather, his mind could. Evolutionarily, these thoughts are meant to keep

Brian on his toes, to keep him striving to be better so he doesn't fall behind and get kicked out of the group. They are not superficial thoughts about boring trainings (the latter being more amenable to disputes than the former).

I'm betting your mind does the same. Check this against your own thinking. How many times have you tried to talk yourself out of thoughts you knew weren't serving you? If disputing a thought works and thus makes you more likely to pursue values-driven activity (i.e., is "workable"), that is great! I like to use disputes when I'm sitting in traffic and it makes the experience more tolerable. But the deeper *I am_____* thoughts seem to work differently. Again, if you're able to convince yourself you're a rock star, and this makes you boldly go in directions you care about, Godspeed! But if you're like Brian and me and this doesn't work, you'll learn the alternative offered in this chapter. This is where instead of working so damn hard to change the *content* of your thinking, you are going to learn to change your *relationship* with it instead. Doing so will build psychological flexibility by preventing thoughts from becoming obstacles to values-based living.

You Get to Choose Whether to Listen

We don't do a lot of thinking about thinking. Thoughts happen and we listen. Your mind says, *The electric bill is due tomorrow,* so you pay it. You think, *A little background music would be lovely right now,* and you stream your favorite artist. It happens automatically, like a cognitive shortcut—no need to waste mental energy hemming and hawing over bills and ballads. But the same automatic process happens when you think, *This is boring; I don't want to do this now—I'll do it later,* and you procrastinate. Or your mind says, *The office party won't be fun*, so you don't go. If meeting deadlines (not procrastinating) and being more connected to colleagues (going to that office party) matter to you, these reactions become what we call unworkable or values incongruent. When you listen to your thoughts without considering whether doing so will move you toward or away from values, you are being psychologically inflexible.

There is a relatively simple (though not easy) fix to this: choosing whether to listen to your thoughts or not. To do so, you must first become aware of your thinking—an active observer. Think of it like being a spectator at a sporting event. You are on the sidelines or in the bleachers—hell, this is an imagery exercise, so go ahead and put yourself up in the luxury box with Beyoncé. No matter where you're watching from, you're doing just that—watching. You're paying close attention, in a curious way, but you're separate from the action. You're invested in what happens; maybe you even cheer on Team Values or jeer at Team Imposter, but you are observing from a distance without jumping into the action.

This then becomes a POP. Remember the Four *P*s from chapter 6? **Pause**, **pick**, and **persist** or **pivot**? We're going to add on here. You've already learned to notice you are at a POP and ask what your choice is in service of (moving toward values or away from discomfort). Now in your **pause**, you are also observing your thoughts. When you **pick**, you are asking, "What are my values in this moment? If I listen to what my mind is saying, will this move me toward or away from those values?" Then you either **persist** if your behavior is *workable* (values consistent) or **pivot** if it's *unworkable* (values inconsistent). When your mind says the electric bill is due tomorrow and you care about the stove remaining functional so you can feed yourself or your family, you'll want to listen to that thought and **persist** in moving forward with the payment. When your mind says the office party won't be fun, but being an active and engaged colleague matters to you, you will **pivot** to attending the party despite what your mind says.

Sometimes this can get complicated, and imposter thoughts are a perfect example. Let's say you want to apply to graduate school or for academic advancement or a new job. When your mind tells you you're not qualified, should you listen? You might think I'm going to say, "No way! Live full-size, not fun-size!" But it's a little more nuanced than this. Let's take this thought through the Four *P*s:

Pause: Take a breath, slow down, and notice the story: *I'm not qualified. Who do I think I am to apply for this?*

Pick: What are your values in this context? Maybe they're courage, willingness (to take a risk, be vulnerable, feel fear and self-doubt), and boldness. But maybe they're also self-knowledge, honesty, and humility.

Persist or Pivot: With all those values front and center, being honest with yourself about your true qualifications and how they match the job description, while also being brave and willing to risk rejection, should you persist with the application, or pivot toward gaining more knowledge or experience?

We crave certainty about right or wrong answers, but life is rarely so simple. This might feel discouraging, but let's bolster your hope a bit with what psychologist Marsha Linehan calls *wise mind*.[3]

Wise Mind

Linehan founded dialectical behavior therapy, an empirically supported therapy designed to help people who struggle with intense emotions. According to Linehan, we have three primary states of mind: emotion mind, rational mind, and wise mind. The emotional side of our brain (figuratively, not anatomically) is responsible for our creativity and feelings of love, excitement, hurt, jealousy, etc. Being in *emotion mind*, though, refers to a state where logical thinking has been hijacked. Planning becomes difficult, and data may be misinterpreted through a lens of upset. The rational side of our brain is responsible for planning, scheduling, paying bills, and attending to facts. *Rational mind*, though, refers to a state of mind that is overly analytical or intellectual, where emotions are disregarded. Being strictly in emotion mind or rational mind has a cost. *Wise mind*, though, is where emotion mind and rational mind intersect.

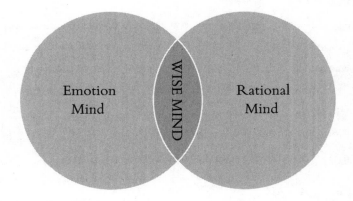

Wise mind combines the logic and facts of rational mind with the feelings of emotion mind to create a space of intuitive knowing. It's that feeling you get when you've considered the pros and cons (rational mind) and attended to your feelings (emotion mind) and arrived at a grounded, gut sense of what to do. When you're not sure whether to persist or pivot, wise mind can help guide you. Wise mind is not always easy to find. There's no magic trick to forcing yourself there. But it can help to think back on times when you have just known the "right" thing to do. You may have still felt uncertainty (because the outcome of any decision is unknown at the time the decision is made), but you had a quiet, centered sense you were making a wise choice.

For me, finding wise mind often means taking a couple of slow, mindful breaths, then asking myself some of the following questions:

- "If I didn't feel anxious or worried, what might I choose?"
- "If I didn't fear the outcome, what would I do?"
- "If no one knew I was doing this, would I still do it?" (This question gets at motivation—am I just trying to impress, or is this truly right for me deep down?)
- "If someone I admire were watching me right now, would I persist or pivot?" (This is not about impression management, but about being accountable for the behavior I choose.)
- "If I'm being truly honest with myself here, what feels really right?"
- "Even if there's a chance it will all go to hell, does this still feel like the right choice right now?"

When you are at a POP and you have gotten clear on your values, try connecting to your wise mind for help in knowing whether to persist or pivot.

RECOGNIZING THE GAP TRAP

A client once came to see me, hoping I could help her lose weight (oh, the irony). She was smart, kind, funny, ambitious, and a great mom. Nonetheless, she felt stuck. She was divorced and wanted to be dating. She felt stagnant at her job and wanted to grow professionally. She was ready and willing but believed she couldn't do either one successfully until her body was a smaller size. She had fallen into the gap trap. The story in her mind went like this: *I will write my online dating profile as soon as I lose fifty pounds. I will start applying for jobs once I'm down to a size 10.* She had evidence—cold, hard data—that proved heavier women were discriminated against in the dating and job markets. Because this story was so compelling and believable, she listened and waited and focused on weight loss instead of on dating and finding a new job. She was *trapped* in a stagnated life because of a perceived *gap* in worth and confidence. And this wasn't a recent or brief struggle for her. She had been listening to these thoughts for *seventeen years.* For nearly two decades she had been putting her dreams on the back burner. Her research evidence wasn't wrong; heavier women are discriminated against—and yet they also have jobs and romantic partners. She knew this but had gotten so hooked by her story and afraid of rejection that her life had been at a standstill for a very long time. Needless to say, our work together focused not on weight-loss goals, but on pursuing a rich and meaningful life at any body size, while also making values-based choices for health.

Consider your own gap traps. What are you waiting to have more or less of before you move forward with values-based choices? For my client, it was less weight and more confidence. With imposterism, it's often one more class, degree, job—some form of knowledge or experience or expertise (especially if you are the Expert version of imposter)—that you tell yourself you need first. The gap trap may be particularly seductive if you have been marginalized. When the cultural models for who deserves a seat at the table are predominantly WHMPs (the white, heterosexual men of privilege we discussed in chapter 1), it can trigger those "I'm not good enough" stories. Of course, you can't change your race, sexual orientation, gender identity, disability status, or history and experience of privilege. And so you may feel compelled to somehow compensate: to be twice as good to be good enough. Thus, you wait. When I was offered the faculty position, I was tempted to turn it down until I took a stats refresher course. I could have stayed *trapped* in my thankless job because I believed I had a *gap* in my expertise.

CLOSING THE GAP

Part of what sets the trap is believing you have to close the gap before you get started. But when you are at a POP and you pause to notice your thoughts, you can see that listening to the "I will do X as soon as Y" story will not result in workable, psychologically flexible action. After seventeen years, or any waiting period, it seems we need an alternative to closing the gap. As we've already talked about in this chapter, this boils down to forging a new relationship with your thoughts. Let's get into a few strategies for doing so.

Go Fly a Kite

I recently took my kids to the park on an unusually blustery day. There were two girls there, maybe six and eight years old, wearing matching sundresses and sandals. They both held kites, and I watched as the older girl started running and at first kept her kite close to her body. As she ran, she gradually let the string out so the kite could climb higher and higher. Once the kite was high in the sky, she stopped running and just let it float high above her head. She glanced at it occasionally, then let her dad anchor the handle so the kite could fly on its own while she spun in circles, then blew bubbles. Then her sister took a turn. She, too, kept her kite close to her body. Only she did not let the string out more than a tiny bit. Within seconds, her kite was tangled in a low-hanging tree branch. She tugged and pulled and yelled and cried as her kite got harder and harder to free from the tree's branches. Thankfully, her tall parents were able to rescue the kite and give her a few pointers on how she might try again.

Watching this scene, I thought, *Huh, this is exactly what happens with thoughts.* When we keep them too close, they get all tangled and steal our attention. But when we create distance, we can watch them dance or even put them down and just do our thing. They don't go away when we put them down—they're still there, hovering above—but we can choose whether and how to attend to them.

Our minds are incredibly powerful. Maybe thinking about kites doesn't sound like an effective way to manage your imposter thoughts. But right now, I want you to imagine an old-school green chalkboard. Imagine you and I are standing at that chalkboard, and I take my very long fingernails and scrape them down the length of the board. What happens? Are your shoulders up at your ears? Is your face scrunched up? Are you feeling mad at me, perhaps? And yet there are no chalkboards in your actual environment (and I have short nails that wouldn't make much of a sound anyway). Think about lemons or pickles, and your mouth will water. Think about someone you adore dying unexpectedly, and you can feel emotions similar to those that would arise should that tragedy actually occur. Our minds are mighty. But in the same way imagining a death can trigger powerful feelings if we get tangled in those thoughts, imagining our thoughts as floating kites can reduce the power of those very same thoughts. The next time you are at a POP and your inner imposter voice shows up, imagine you can place those thoughts on a kite and gradually let that kite float up into the sky. Importantly, the kite isn't going away, and neither are your thoughts. But getting some distance will put you in a position to observe the thoughts without getting tangled, pick your values, and persist or pivot to a workable choice.

Oh, Sheila

I'm not sure exactly how it began, but a few years back, whenever my inner critic and inner imposter voice popped up, I started answering with "Pipe down, Sheila—I've got this!" If your name is Sheila, I mean no offense. I don't know any Sheilas except the one from the song "Oh Sheila" (which I apologize for getting stuck in your head if you're of a certain age). Perhaps this seems too twee, but in actuality, naming thoughts is a technique for detaching from and observing them—for not getting hooked. Dan Siegel, one of the authors of *The Whole-Brain Child*, says you have to "name it to tame it."[4] At POPs, naming that inner voice creates space from which you can choose to pivot to a workable alternative. To be clear, telling Sheila to pipe down was not a way to get her to shut up. I would if I could, but we all know by now that doesn't work, right? The phrase was more my shorthand way of telling the thoughts they didn't get to dictate what I was going to choose.

Let's name yours. I've had clients choose things like Big Bully, Fake News, the Despot, and Bill (this is my favorite because it's my husband's name. Pipe down, Bill!). You can give yours a regular person name like Sheila or Bill, or a title like the Mind Demon. There's no right or wrong here, and if you notice you're struggling to come up with the perfect choice, see if you can hold that lightly and let something gently rise to the top. Email me or post it on social media and tag me. I'd love to hear what you come up with! And if you get stuck, I'll try to come up with one with you.

Clouds Versus Fog

One morning, my kids and I woke up to a thick fog blanketing our neighborhood. Driving to school, we could barely see the brake lights of the car in front of us. We worried out loud about a teenager riding his bicycle in the street. My kids adorably educated me about how clouds and fog are really the same thing, only in a different position relative to where we are—with fog, we're basically standing in the middle of a cloud. Like the kite-flying girls, this inspired me to think about thoughts too. When we're hooked by the content of our thoughts, it's like we're standing in the fog, surrounded on all sides, barely able to see anything other than the fog itself. We need to move cautiously, aware of potential dangers. When we're not hooked—when we're detached and observing our thoughts— it's like we're watching the clouds, standing rooted to the ground, looking up at them high in the sky, distant and separate. We can observe their qualities—color, texture, rate of movement—without being affected by them. At a point of possibility, when you pause, notice whether you have been enveloped on all sides by your inner critic and imposter thoughts, acting cautiously to avoid danger, and imagine you can gather the fog and place it up in the sky in cloud form. Observe the clouds as they move across the sky—observe your thoughts as they move across your mind. Allow this to create a space where you are better positioned to pick your values and persist or pivot to a values-driven choice.

Reel Memes Are a GIF(T)

Occasionally, when I'm scrolling through social media, I'll click on a reel that looks cute or funny. Many times, I'm expecting to hear a young mom say something about her cute baby, or a dog owner talk about his puppy. But then a creepy robot voice narrates the action instead of the reel maker using their own voice. It strikes me as a perfect way to practice creating a new relationship with the inner imposter. Normally, you probably hear your own voice in your head telling you you're a fraud. See what happens if you repeat those thoughts in a creepy robot-like voice. Better yet, go to a free text-to-speech website like www.texttospeechrobot.com, and plug your thoughts right in. You don't have to post them to social media, but I'd love to see it if you do! Or try making a meme or a GIF. Maybe a "most interesting man in the world" meme, like "I don't always go after what I want, but when I do, I'm sure I'll be exposed for the fraud I really am."

This may sound like a minimizing of what can be a very painful internal experience. And in a way, it is. Our thoughts don't have superpowers—they are sounds and syllables and images that have power only if we give it to them. So how can we take away their power? By not taking them so seriously. Getting playful with our thinking is like kryptonite to the inner imposter. Give it a shot right now. Take one of your old painful thoughts or stories that give you trouble. Now imagine Homer Simpson saying it with a "D'oh!" at the end. Or imagine Mariah Carey singing it in her highest octave. Or your bilingual friend or Google translate saying it in a language you don't understand. The words have remained the same, but the meaning and power have shifted. At points of possibility, this shift creates a context where flexible choice is more freely available. The next time you come across a funny reel, meme, or GIF, imagine how you might incorporate a thought you typically take too seriously. Notice what happens to that thought's power.

Listening to self-limiting beliefs as if they are dictums we must follow leads to psychologically inflexible behavior. Workable action is more likely when we become curious observers of our thoughts and see them for what they are: letters or images strung together in ways that may *feel* compelling but don't have any actual power. At points of possibility, we get to choose how to respond to our thoughts. Watching them like floating kites, naming them, turning fog thoughts into cloud thoughts, and getting playful with them can help create space where picking values and persisting or pivoting becomes more accessible. Thoughts are only half of the equation of what threatens to keep us stuck in unworkable action. Uncomfortable feelings (emotions, sensations, urges) and the allure of the comfort zone are the other.

The Recap: What to Know

- How we think about a situation affects how we feel. It can affect what we do if we let it.
- Changing thoughts is desirable only if it works by moving you toward values-consistent action.
- When changing thoughts doesn't work, you can change your relationship with thoughts. Observe them and choose whether listening will result in workable action.
- Contact wise mind to help with decisions to persist or pivot.
- Beware the gap trap: getting trapped in stagnation due to a perceived gap in knowledge, experience, expertise, or confidence.

The Work: What to Do

- Choose when to listen to thoughts and when to simply observe in a distanced, curious manner.
- Name your imposter voice.
- Let thoughts out like a kite.
- Turn fog thoughts into cloud thoughts.
- Get playful with thoughts.

Chapter 9

Fear, Self-Doubt, Shame, and the Allure of the Comfort Zone

Life is pain, Highness. Anyone who says differently is selling something.
—*Westley,* The Princess Bride

When my first book came out, I was invited to an author dinner by my publisher. The invitation came electronically, so I could see the full list of invitees. Steve Hayes, Kelly Wilson, Robyn Walser, Kirk Strosahl. These names will mean nothing to you if you're not an ACT person or involved in the community, but they were gods to me. My professional heroes. I immediately started to hyperventilate and burst into uncontrollable sobs. I was flooded with panic and imposter feelings. I seriously considered declining the invitation, telling myself I'd try again next year, once I had a little more experience and confidence under my belt (hello, Expert Imposter sitting in the gap trap). But with the date of the dinner months away, I called up the courage to click the "Will Attend" button from the safety of my living room, knowing I could always change my mind.

On the evening of the dinner, I would have sacrificed my firstborn for a Valium. OK, that's a slight exaggeration, but it was truly the most anxious I'd ever been for a professional event. I debated backing out, knowing the only way to get relief from the intense anxiety I was experiencing was to bail. Instead, I forged ahead, gulping down a glass of wine in my hotel room and begging my husband not to leave my side.

When we arrived at the restaurant, the invited guests were directed to an outdoor patio to have pre-dinner cocktails. I started chatting with Matt McKay, a well-known ACT psychologist and prolific writer. He was also the person listed on the electronic invitation as the party's host. We introduced ourselves, and I asked him how he came to be the host of the event. He looked at me like I had four heads. "Uh, because I own the publishing company?" he replied.

As if I wasn't already anxious enough about being exposed as an incompetent fraud, I had just shoved my foot so far down my throat, I thought I might suffocate on the spot. I had no idea Matt McKay was the owner of the company that had published my book.

We laughed, I blushed (a lot), then he asked, "So who are you?" If I had blurted out the first thought that came to mind, I would have responded, "Oh, I'm nobody." Luckily, I took a beat and instead explained that I had coauthored *The Big Book of ACT Metaphors* with Niloo Afari. McKay, much to my relief and joy, gushed about how pleased he was with the book.

At that point we were instructed to head inside to the dining room, where we were seated for dinner. The cocktails and colorful language flowed. With every jovial curse word uttered by my colleagues, I felt more and more at home. We talked shop, but we also talked about our families, our travels, and our plans for the future.

What started as panic, self-doubt, and an embarrassing foot-in-mouth situation turned into one of the most fun and fulfilling nights I have ever had. The following year, when I was invited to the dinner again, I was still nervous, but a little less so. I knew some folks and thought I could probably hold my own. By the third year, I was calling my professional heroes my friends.

FIRE VERSUS BURNT TOAST

Consider a time you experienced intense anxiety, panic, self-doubt, or imposterism. What did you do? Maybe you didn't click "Will Attend" on your invitation. Maybe you clicked "Screw It" and avoided whatever was causing the feelings. If so, you did exactly what your body is built to do: protect you from danger. From a biological and evolutionary standpoint, our only real jobs as humans are to survive and procreate. So we are built with a threat-detection system to help us do just that. If you're driving and suddenly hear brakes loudly screeching, you will likely experience a fear response—racing heart, shortness of breath, lightheadedness. This is what happens when your sympathetic nervous system is activated to help you react appropriately to a potentially dangerous situation. You will probably hit your brakes, look around, and check your mirrors to quickly assess the situation before driving on. Sudden, unexpected airplane turbulence can trigger a similar response. Your body is reacting to a potential threat. Once the pilot comes on to reassure you the bumps are nothing to worry about, the parasympathetic nervous system kicks in to help calm you down.

A fear response in the face of actual danger prepares us to fight, flee, or freeze so we might have our best chance at survival (for a more extensive explanation of anxiety, fear/panic, worry, stress, and our body's physical, emotional, cognitive, and behavioral responses, see the first chapter of my book *Be Mighty*). Only our threat-detection system isn't strictly concerned with the presence of physical, life-or-death threats; it also keeps on the lookout for social threats. And in the case of both physical and social danger, our bodies and minds can react as if we were experiencing a true threat even when a situation is safe. It's like having your smoke alarm go off—sometimes there's an actual fire; many times you merely burned your toast. Our bodies don't always know the difference.

When I was invited to the publisher dinner, my body and mind responded in much the same way they would have if Matt McKay had held a knife to my throat. The social situation *felt* threatening, but Matt McKay is a nice guy. Why did it feel so threatening? Because it mattered to me so much. I wanted nothing more than to be accepted by this group of brilliant, high-achieving individuals who shared many of my same values. I didn't want to be outed as a fraud and kicked out of the club. As we've discussed, this fear has evolutionary roots, and today our limbic systems have not evolved to reliably differentiate perceived threat from actual danger.

This means that we can rely on our sense of danger to keep us safe when it tells us to avoid swimming in thirty-foot waves, jumping off a two-story building, or getting too close to a campfire. But if we rely on it every time we feel scared and avoid accordingly, it may bring us relief from fear, but that relief will also come at great cost. If screeching tires and turbulence, both of which turned out to be safe, resulted in you giving up driving and flying, you might reduce your fear in the moment but at the expense of your freedom. If I had declined my publisher's dinner invitation, I would have immediately cured my in-the-moment panic and imposter feelings. But I also would have sacrificed fun, fulfillment, friendship, and the opportunity to make important professional connections. What's more, I would have taught myself the best way to get relief from fear in the future is to avoid whatever is causing it. In other words, avoidance begets more avoidance, often shrinking our lives further and further as time goes on.

EXPERIENTIAL AVOIDANCE

Emotional pain is the price of admission to being human. Not one of us gets to escape it. But oh, how we try. No one *wants* to feel uncomfortable, but when we rely strictly on our desire for comfort, we often sacrifice our values. We trade workability for psychological inflexibility. In my example above, my panic and imposter feelings weren't my problem. It was my desire to avoid feeling them that threatened to keep me living fun-size. *I had to be open to experiencing the feelings in order to live full-size.* Granted, I cheated a little at first when I downed the glass of wine in my hotel room and clung to my husband. Nobody's perfect. But I didn't drink so much that I made a fool of myself; nor did I shut down and shy away from talking to the people who intimidated me. As we discussed in chapter 4, the idea that pain is not the problem, and it is our unwillingness to have it that keeps us stuck, has been summed up by Buddhists as pain × resistance = suffering. Pain, for humans, is a given, a constant. But resistance is where we often have the power to choose a new response and decrease emotional suffering.

Consider what really holds you back and keeps you small. Is it your fear and imposterism? Or how you respond when they show up? Often, in an effort to feel less anxiety, self-doubt, or other uncomfortable emotions, we engage in experiential avoidance (EA).

> Experiential avoidance is anything we do or don't do to feel less of what we don't want or more of what we do and to prevent feared outcomes from occurring.[1]

Examples of EA include situational avoidance, substance use, distraction (like social media and binge-watching shows), lashing out, perfectionism, procrastination, isolation, or compulsive gambling, sex, or shopping. In the next chapter, we'll look at five main categories of EA. Like the subtypes of imposters, you may engage in various types of EA but will likely have one as your main go-to.

It Works or You Wouldn't Do It

You may look at the list of EA examples above and say, "Ugh, avoidance is so bad. Why do I do this to myself?" We all do this to ourselves because avoidance works! Feeling irritated at your kids or coworkers? Yell at them to knock it off or get their shit together. Instant release. Feeling stressed at the end of a long day? Pour a glass or two of wine. Alcohol is a central nervous system depressant that will quickly reduce feelings of anxiety. Feeling self-doubt and fear you'll be revealed as a fraud? Stay late at work and go, go, go, do, do, do. Feel safe that maybe you won't be outed today.

The behaviors we choose have a purpose, a function. They bring some type of relief from pain and sometimes add a little dopamine to boot. It's hard to resist the allure of that comfort zone. Comfort zones are, well, comfortable. But avoidance has costs.

When you drink too much, the relief you feel today results in double the anxiety plus a headache and irritability tomorrow. When you snap at your kids or coworkers, you sacrifice your reputation and your relationships. When you overachieve, you risk burnout and never really outrun imposterism. Importantly, these costs are often tied directly to values.

Check out the table below, and add two or three examples from your own personal experience.

It Works (Until It Doesn't)

Discomfort	Experiential Avoidance	It Works! (The Function)	Until It Doesn't (the Cost)
Anxiety	Drink alcohol	Feel relief and relaxation in the short term	Results in double the anxiety, headache, irritability, guilt about drinking too much
Irritability	Snap, yell	Feel release in the moment; feel in control or a sense of power	Damages relationships and reputation
Self-doubt, imposterism	Overwork, overachieve	Feel more in control temporarily, and like you won't be revealed as a fraud	Leads to burnout and doesn't cure imposter feelings in the long term

The Path of Least Resistance

When my husband's grandmother fell ill, his cousins urged him to get on a flight quickly. Billy was distraught. He was about to lose his beloved gram and felt overwhelmed by the list of tasks he would need to complete to make the red-eye within a matter of hours. He put it off and booked his flight for a few days later—and didn't make it in time to see his grandmother before she passed. He was flooded with guilt and regret. Packing for the trip back east, now to attend funeral services, he haphazardly threw things in a suitcase, saying, "Screw it. If I need anything, I'll just buy it when I get there." When he got there, he didn't have a suit for the funeral. This meant spending an entire day and a *lot* of money to find a suit and get it tailored the same day. In just three days, an understandably strong pull to avoid short-term pain resulted in far greater suffering.

Economists refer to the tendency to choose short-term benefit over long-term gain as *present bias*.[2] Nobel Prize–winning psychologist Daniel Kahneman calls it a *general law of least effort*,[3] and behavioral scientist Katy Milkman refers to it simply as *impulsivity*.[4] In essence, if there are multiple ways of achieving a goal, humans will opt for the least demanding course of action to get there. Whatever you call it, the path of least resistance is a very common form of EA.

Akin to the examples in the "It Works (Until It Doesn't)" table above, the path of least resistance feels good. It provides relief. Temporarily. Until it results in longer-term cost. Feeling dread about working on a project? Put it off until later. Procrastination is an instant fix for Project Dread. Feeling scared to share your feelings with a friend or partner? Keep them to yourself—problem solved! No risk of rejection or feelings of vulnerability now. Feeling self-doubt and fear you'll be revealed as a fraud? Just wait to go after the promotion or new job until next year. Phew, crisis averted! You won't be found out today. But of course, putting a task off today means the same amount of work tomorrow, with less time to meet your deadline. Yesterday's fix for dread leads to double the dread today. Shutting down self-expression with friends feels safe today but robs your relationships of intimacy and puts you at greater risk of rejection down the road. Avoiding professional challenges may make you feel less like a fraud in the short term, but it shrinks your professional life in the long run. The path of least resistance may offer a temporary shortcut to the comfort zone, but it often leads away from values and circles, straight back to pain.

Ego Depletion

When I wait until the end of the day to exercise, it almost never happens. Instead, I end up lumping out in front of the TV and snacking even when I'm not hungry. If you find yourself more vulnerable to the path of least resistance and EA at the end of a physically, emotionally, or cognitively taxing day, you are not alone. Psychologist Roy Baumeister calls this phenomenon *ego depletion*. He demonstrated in several experiments that our ability to self-regulate acts as a limited resource that is depleted as we face successive challenges.[5] The belief that self-control is limited is a strong one in psychology. But in his book *Indistractable*, Nir Eyal encourages readers to rethink this idea, calling ego depletion theory "one of the most pervasive bits of folk psychology."[6] This is because researchers who have dug into Baumeister's findings a bit more deeply have suggested his studies may have been inaccurately interpreted.[7] Carol Dweck, who became well known for her research on growth mindset, tested Baumeister's ego depletion theory and concluded that the only participants for whom self-control was a limited resource were those who *believed* self-control was a limited resource.[8] As Eyal points out, if Dweck's conclusions are accurate, then we must stop perpetuating the idea that self-control is a limited resource. If ego depletion is really a problem with thinking, then we must address the thinking.

If, when encountering POPs—like whether to complete boring paperwork, get on your Peloton, or make a healthy food choice—you find yourself pivoting like a boss to values-congruent choices in the morning but regressing to EA over the course of the day, either ego depletion or your belief in ego depletion *may* be to blame. This can look like a nighttime loss of self-control around food or alcohol, failing to act patiently with the people in your life, or being more likely to procrastinate.

Either way, the antidote to EA, the path of least resistance, ego depletion, or erroneous beliefs about ego depletion is a combination of three things:

1. Being present and aware of your thoughts and feelings, which we discussed in chapter 4
2. Keeping your why close by—remaining deeply connected to values, which we discussed in chapters 5 and 6
3. Practicing willingness, which I touch on below and delve into more deeply in chapter 11

Could You Be Wearing Any More Clothes?

EA is like the episode of *Friends* where Joey puts on all of Chandler's clothes ("Look at me—I'm Chandler. Could I *be* wearing any more clothes?") in retaliation for Chandler hiding all of Joey's underwear.[9] We use EA to create layer upon layer of perceived protection. And like Joey, underneath all those layers, we're naked. It can feel impossible to allow our naked selves to be exposed, to risk that level of vulnerability. But wearing all those clothes is terribly restricting (not to mention sweaty). Think back to when you were young, before self-consciousness took hold. Imagine a time you went skinny-dipping or ran away from a trusted caregiver after a bath, and connect with how free you felt.

Right now, I'm remembering a video of me wearing a bikini when I was maybe seven or eight years old. It was probably the last time I ever wore one. In the video, I'm with my cousin, and we are dancing and bouncing, trying to position our silly selves front and center for the camera. Our limbs are flailing in every direction; our heads are bopping side to side. We were exposed and totally free to move our bodies in any and every direction we chose.

Letting go of EA can be like that. As adults, the traps of language have developed (rules, assumptions, judgments, predictions, rationalizations), and so we likely don't *feel* as free as we did when we were kids. But when we're willing to remove the layers that feel protective but are restricting our movements, we free our bodies and voices to express themselves authentically and in accordance with our values. I'm not sure I'll ever *literally* do a silly dance in front of a video camera in a bikini again, but I'd sure like to do it figuratively in the areas of my personal and professional life that deeply matter to me.

Shame

When you imagine shedding layers of protection and being exposed, what feelings do you notice? In addition to an overall vulnerability, what else arises when you imagine being truly, unapologetically, 100 percent you? I'm guessing there's fear, maybe dread. But I wonder if there might be some shame in there too.

Human beings are evolutionarily wired for connection and belonging. Time and time again, research has shown the single most powerful predictor of overall health and well-being is the presence of quality relationships.[10] When we consider shedding our layers of protective clothing, standing naked in our lives, it can feel like those very connections are at stake. *What will they say or do if I really, really let them see me?* We may fear rejection or abandonment, or if we feel inadequate, unworthy, or unlovable, we may experience shame. If you have a history of marginalization, as many who struggle with imposterism do, shame can arise as an emotional component of being stigmatized.[11] And shame is an experience humans work very hard to escape or avoid.[12]

In her book *Dare to Lead*, Brené Brown describes shame as a fear of disconnection. She says, "Shame is the intensely painful feeling or experience of believing that we're flawed and therefore unworthy of love, belonging, and connection."[13] When we hide beneath those protective layers, we avoid feeling unworthy and escape feelings of shame. The avoidance works in the short term to give us a sense of psychological safety. But hiding our true selves from others ultimately reduces our access to love and belonging and makes disconnection more likely. With imposterism, we often keep our fears of inadequacy close to the vest so as not to reveal ourselves as frauds. We suffer in silence in service of belonging and to avoid shame but end up further alienating ourselves, creating greater disconnection and loneliness.[14]

Connection and belonging arise when we are willing to be figuratively naked with each other (and maybe literally, but I don't recommend that in professional settings). Intimacy stems from vulnerability.[15] From shedding our protective layers and showing one another our true selves—wounds, warts, and all. Perfection does not breed connection—openness about our very human flaws does. Check this against your experience. Consider a moment of connection you've experienced with another human: What was the context? Did it arise when you spent time in their perfectly immaculate home, where their straight-A, athletic musician kids were cooperating quietly after you all shared a three-course, home-cooked, organic gourmet dinner? I'm betting not.

When Denise was a postdoctoral fellow in psychology, she reached out to ask me for career advice after feeling inspired by a talk I gave to her cohort. We exchanged several professional emails over the years, consulting with one another on everything from finding office space to maternity leaves and client referrals. After seven years of emails, I moved to the town next to hers, and Denise initiated an in-person meeting to consult about her goal of starting a private therapy practice. This meeting blossomed into frequent beach walks and getting our families together. Our conversations began to transform from just talking about business to also talking about marriage, working parenthood, raising kids with special needs, extended family, struggles, and dreams.

I'll never forget visiting Denise's home for the first time. She didn't clean the house before my arrival and simply offered a casual apology for the mess. I never loved her more than in that moment. I adored that she trusted me to see the true state of her home. If her house, unlike mine, had been immaculate, I would have felt unworthy and inadequate. I would have hidden under my own layers of protective clothing to avoid shame and disconnection, paradoxically creating a perfect context to threaten our bond. Instead, I knew from that moment it was safe for us to be real with one another. It was a true moment of connection. Consider a moment of connection of your own—one that stemmed from shedding protective layers and allowing exposure and vulnerability. Who were you with? What happened? How did it feel?

It may seem strange that I'm writing about personal connections in a book for professionals. But if you look to your experience, I think you will find that much of your own EA—personally and professionally—may stem from shame and fear of disconnection.

What is at the root of the fear of being exposed as a fraud? That others will see you for who you fear you really are, and if they do, they will reject and abandon you. You'll be ousted from the group you desperately want to belong to.

The goal of this chapter is to help you see your patterns of EA. In chapter 11, we'll talk in detail about how to change your relationship with fear, shame, imposterism, and whatever other uncomfortable feelings arise, so they no longer hold you back from pursuing bold action.

SHELLEY THE PERFECTIONIST

For years, Shelley excelled at managing law firms and real estate offices. She oversaw a staff of ten to fifteen people and supported four executives at a time. She taught herself new high-level skills. But because she didn't have an advanced degree, she didn't value any of her accomplishments. She was also raised to believe that women must marry men, that those men will take care of them, and that she wasn't smart enough to succeed on her own.

Despite her lack of confidence, or perhaps because of it, Shelley opted to pursue not one, not two, but three degrees, and although she was accepted into a competitive doctoral program in psychology, she constantly felt like she was letting herself down. She would get grades back and focus on mistakes or areas needing improvement even when she had performed well on assignments. In her clinical work, she would focus on minor perceived mistakes that had no bearing on the clients. Shelley also compared herself to everyone—including people who had been in practice for over a decade—holding herself to the same standards despite still being a student.

She did all of this while raising two children, and instead of patting herself on the back for being able to juggle so much successfully, she hyperfocused on the laundry that wasn't getting done and the clients who weren't progressing as much as she thought they should (all the while asking herself, *Why do they keep coming back to me? Don't they know I'm a fraud?*). When she was accepted to the best psychology master's program in Australia (she already had a doctorate but needed the master's to see clients), she was certain they had made a mistake or had given her a spot out of pity.

As a Perfectionist Imposter, to compensate for her constant fear of being revealed as incompetent, Shelley held herself to extremely high standards. These helped her succeed—she even had her thesis accepted with no revisions (for anyone who's never done a thesis or dissertation, this is truly unheard of)—but no amount of perfectionism ever fixed her imposter feelings. Shelley chalked her successes up to other people's errors or them "just being nice" or going easy on her. It worked…until it didn't, and she was always on the cusp of burnout. If Shelley completed an "It Works (Until It Doesn't)" table, it would look something like this:

Discomfort	Experiential Avoidance	It Works! (The Function)	Until It Doesn't (the Cost)
Low confidence, insecurity	Pursue multiple degrees	Increased sense of control Hope that confidence will improve	Takes time, money, effort Doesn't work to cure insecurity in the long term Having a doctorate increases imposterism in my master's program, because I should know more
Disappointment (in self)	Focus on mistakes and perceived failures Compare self to others	Sense that I can improve and better myself Belief it helps avoid future mistakes and failures	Leads to feeling sad, dejected, inadequate, and more disappointed in the long term
Imposterism and fear of being found out	Dismiss success Be a perfectionist	Good performance Temporary relief of fear	Takes time and effort Increases stress Creates standards that are impossible to achieve, so I feel more like a failure Doesn't work to cure fear in the long term

Despite these incredibly painful internal experiences and a good dose of EA along the way, Shelley forged ahead with her career. Her pivot out of the corporate world and into mental health arose from a deep desire to help humans during their times of suffering. She was connected to her values of being helpful, supportive, and of service. She recognized she would have to change her relationship with her inner critic and imposter thoughts, observing them in a detached and dispassionate way without letting them be in charge of her choices, so she could boldly pursue her dreams. She chose to move out of her comfort zone and make space for fear, disappointment, and insecurity in service of living full-size.

Shelley is now a fully licensed psychologist living her career dream of working in private practice in an acreage setting, surrounded by trees, animals, and supportive colleagues who share her passion for helping others to have a better life through connection, support, and living a life that matters. Shelley cultivated her own psychological flexibility so she could help others do the same. Recently, Shelley stepped even deeper into her clinical role by stepping out of other roles that were not fulfilling or values aligned. While drawing boundaries triggered a fear of disappointing colleagues, she chose to do so anyway. She told me, "It was so liberating to make this decision and know it was one hundred percent right for me."

NOT ALL AVOIDANCE IS "BAD"

While EA can lead to unworkable action, not all EA is problematic. For example, I woke up this morning feeling a great deal of physiological anxiety. I took my kids to school, as I do every day, then headed to yoga. After yoga, my anxiety was gone. Does this make practicing yoga an example of EA? It served to reduce a feeling I didn't want to have, so yes, it counts as EA. Is that a problem? *It depends* on whether it came at a cost. It took about two hours out of my schedule (getting into yoga clothes, driving to the studio, taking the seventy-five-minute class, driving home, showering, and dressing in work clothes) and cost fifteen dollars. I had two hours to spare today, I can afford fifteen dollars, and it didn't take me away from other values-based activities. My kids were at school, and I had plenty of time left in my day to write. I also care about connecting with my yoga community and taking care of my body. So while practicing yoga changed my internal experience, it came at minimal cost, with no cost to my values. The meditative nature of the practice also put me in a better space to write, which is consistent with my value of creativity. In this instance, yoga as avoidance was not problematic. However, if I were so unwilling to feel anxious that I spent two hours every evening taking yoga classes during the only time I have to spend with my family (which matters to me), this would then become avoidance with a cost and would therefore be unworkable.

There are also times you will *choose* avoidance, and that's OK too. What I hope is that you will do so with your eyes wide open—that it will be a conscious, deliberate choice, rather than one that just occurs on autopilot. For example, you have reports to write at the end of an especially taxing day, and you choose procrastination as a form of self-care while making a commitment to tackle them tomorrow. Or you're prioritizing healthy living by reducing your sugar or alcohol consumption, but when your best friend gets married, you make a choice to eat wedding cake and drink champagne in service of celebration.

EA comes in all shapes and sizes and can even be cleverly disguised (as in the second part of the yoga example above). In the years I've been specializing in ACT, anxiety, and imposterism, I have identified five main sorts of EA. You will likely recognize yourself and your behavior in more than one of these categories, but you will probably have a main go-to, which we will identify in chapter 10.

The Recap: What to Know

- Emotional pain is not the problem; everything you do to avoid it is what keeps you stuck.
- Experiential avoidance (EA) is anything you do or don't do to feel less of what you don't want or more of what you do.
- EA works to provide relief in the short term but often comes at a cost, especially in relation to values.
- Shame, fear of disconnection, and the path of least resistance may lie at the root of much EA.
- Not all EA is problematic—the question is whether it comes at a cost.

The Work: What to Do

- Complete an "It Works (Until It Doesn't)" table to understand your own patterns of avoidance, including the function and cost of your avoidance behaviors.

Chapter 10

The Five Sorts of Avoidance

Avoidance has never been a great tactic in solving any problem. For most situations in life, not addressing what's going on only makes matters worse.

—*Luvvie Ajayi Jones*

"*Bzzzzzz.*" My husband buzzed at me from the sofa as I flitted about our apartment. It was late on a Saturday morning, before we were married and had kids. He was still in his pj's, rewatching a Marvel movie. I had finished graduate school so was no longer required to do homework on weekends. In other words, I could have been relaxing on the sofa, snuggled up to Billy. Instead, I was making myself busy with I don't remember what—anything to Just. Keep. Going. This was my avoidance strategy. I had spent so long in school, where there was always too much to do and never enough time to do it, that I couldn't sit still without feeling anxious about all the things I "should" be accomplishing. Even though I had graduated and my situation had changed, my thoughts and feelings hadn't caught up. To manage my anxiety and quiet my mind, I would go, go, go, do, do, do. It made me feel productive and in control. My to-do list was my best friend, and nothing gave me a rush quite like checking tasks off it. This strategy had been effective for succeeding in school but came at a cost when I was no longer able to just sit and be. It meant missing opportunities to quietly connect with the people I cared most about. It meant not being able to practice what I was preaching when I would recommend meditation to my clients but avoid it in my own life. While go-go-going and do-do-doing allowed me to avoid the anxiety associated with sitting still, it replaced that anxiety with a constant sense of urgency and leaning into whatever was next. I was like that old cartoon character the Tasmanian Devil, spinning through my life at full speed, surrounded by a swirl of chaos.

I call myself and others who engage in this type of avoidance the Doers. In my twenty years as a practicing mental health professional and anxiety specialist, I have discovered that harmful forms of avoidance can be categorized into five main types: the Doer, the Hider, the Pulsive, the Otherer, and the Thinker. You likely engage in all these types of avoidance here and there, but one will be your main strategy.

In chapter 9, we discussed avoidance in detail—the ways it works (i.e., why you do it) and the cost at which it comes. Identifying the function of your avoidance behaviors will help you spot patterns so you can make new, more workable choices. In this chapter, we'll take the understanding of your EA to another level by identifying your go-to avoidance tactic. Awareness of what you're doing or not doing when emotional pain and imposterism arise is a critical step to changing behavior and becoming more psychologically flexible.

THE DOER

Doers are all about staying busy. They often avoid emotional pain and difficult thoughts by being so active there's no space to experience them. The Doer's mode is "go, go, go, do, do, do." You will often find a Doer making lists, running around accomplishing the tasks on the list, and relishing checking items off the list. If your Doer instinct is particularly strong, you might even put things on your to-do list *after* you've already completed them, just to experience the satisfaction of checking them off. Doers tend to be overpreparers, workaholics, and those who pursue endless knowledge, skills, certificates, and degrees as a way to avoid feeling inadequate. Doers may also engage in things that appear productive, like hobbies or "self-care," but that often serve as sneaky forms of avoidance. For example, a Doer might prefer to play golf or get a mani-pedi during time off because it feels more productive and less like a waste of time than resting. Doers are sensitive to the idea of wasting time and rarely rest.

THE HIDER

When our son, William, was little, he went through an epic stage of constant tantrums. He was nearly kicked out of preschool after he ripped the soldered wrought-iron legs off his teacher's stool. He regularly put jewelry in the full diaper pail, and dolls and electronics in the toilet. He often ripped the sheets off his bed, and all his shirts off their hangers. It's funny to look back on now, but at the time he was very hard to parent. Feeling frustrated and utterly powerless, my husband took to spending more and more time in his office on his computer. It provided a much-needed respite (it worked, or he wouldn't have done it), but it also left me alone to deal with our li'l devil and of course hindered their father-son relationship. Our marriage and his relationship with his kids matter to him more than anything, yet Billy's struggle to tolerate his very understandable distress undermined the things he valued most. Thankfully, both William and his dad have found more psychologically flexible ways to relate to their big feelings, and everyone's relationships have improved as a result.

Billy is the Hider. The Hider is the opposite of the Doer and is a person who seeks comfort by remaining unseen. When difficult emotions like fear, uncertainty, anger, dread, insecurity, or imposterism arise, Hiders escape pain by shutting down, going quiet, being passive, procrastinating, isolating, and avoiding situations that trigger discomfort. They often distract themselves with things like browsing social media, binge-watching TV, playing video games, reading, or taking naps. Hiders find solace in comfort zones but at the expense of relationships, work, and school. They may take on tasks, but if they struggle to complete them, they will fail to communicate this for fear of being judged or letting others down. This lack of communication creates the exact outcome—being negatively evaluated—they are trying to avoid.

THE PULSIVE

"Jay" was a client whose first session with me was on the anniversary of a serious suicide attempt. Jay had had a very difficult childhood, and he had a history of trauma. He never learned how to effectively manage his intense emotional pain, so he resorted to self-harm, violence toward others, compulsions, impulsive tattooing and piercing, and substance abuse. These behaviors offered Jay a quick fix for his immense pain but interfered tremendously in his life, regularly landing him in the hospital, in jail, and without meaningful relationships, all of which increased his pain over time. With therapy, Jay was able to slowly reduce these behaviors, resulting in fewer hospitalizations and incarcerations.

Jay is the Pulsive. Pulsives seek relief from discomfort through compulsive and impulsive behaviors like using substances, shopping, skin picking, cutting, eating, gambling, having sex, hair pulling, nail biting, counting, checking, or other rituals. Pulsives may also lash out verbally or physically when angered or frustrated. Typically, emotional distress involves a tension or urgency that is relieved by the Pulsive's behavior. While compulsive and impulsive behaviors provide a temporary sense of relief and perceived control, they often result in a lower sense of control over time, as the need to engage in these behaviors increases, and the relief they provide decreases.

THE OTHERER

Whenever Jenny is invited out to dinner or a movie, she always defers to what other people want to eat or see. When I interviewed her, she said, "It's just kind of ingrained in me—my first instinct is to look outward in almost all my decisions." She wondered if her opinions were even really her own when it came to music, politics, or other likes and dislikes, because she rarely takes time to digest information before asking others for their opinions. Relying on others gives Jenny comfort in several ways: she feels good making other people happy, she avoids making "wrong" decisions (those that might make her or others unhappy), and she escapes the fear that the people she cares about will abandon her if her choices or opinions differ from theirs. The cost, though, is that Jenny misses out on opportunities to try new things. She also lacks confidence and a sense of self-efficacy, because she hasn't had direct experience making choices or sharing opinions in the absence of her feared consequences occurring. In other words, her belief that others will be unhappy or will stop being her friend is maintained because her avoidance behavior limits access to experiential evidence that would show otherwise. Jenny's dad died recently after a long battle with dementia. She realized her tendency to focus on others' needs—like helping her mom through her grief—runs so deep that she doesn't stop to process her own emotional experiences. She avoids her feelings by focusing on the feelings of others.

Jenny is the Otherer. The Otherer relies on others to facilitate pain avoidance. They do this by reassurance seeking, people-pleasing, or being a follower rather than a leader. Otherers avoid choosing the movie or restaurant and prefer that others decide. When they must decide, Otherers ask for a lot of input before making decisions. This might take the form of online research (with the internet serving as the more knowledgeable "other") or asking multiple friends, family members, or coworkers for opinions. In this way, the Otherer avoids making a "wrong" decision or being judged or negatively evaluated. For similar reasons, they have a difficult time being assertive, saying no, and setting boundaries. They may also overattend to others' needs, often at the expense of their own, and may find themselves apologizing excessively even when it's not warranted. Sometimes, the Otherer's pendulum may swing: over time, passivity and people-pleasing can turn from kind accommodation to angry resentment. This may negatively impact relationships. Likewise, if the Otherer's reassurance seeking becomes excessive, this may also place a burden on relationships.

THE THINKER

After Annabelle graduated from her master's degree program, she was invited to an annual alumni reunion. She was pretty sure she wanted to attend, as it would mean a lot to her to see her former classmates. But instead of immediately committing with a "yes" RSVP, she engaged in weeks of mental gymnastics, asking herself many questions, trying to think through all the logistics and pros and cons. Here are some of the things her mind spun: *I'm going to be away the weekend before—do I want to be gone two weekends in a row? Is it OK to leave the dog again? Where will I stay? How long will I stay? Who's going to be there? Should I share a room? What about COVID? The cost of gas has gotten outrageous, and it's a pretty long drive.* Annabelle felt the need to work through every possible detail. This gave her a short-term sense of control, as if she were preparing and problem-solving so she wouldn't be caught off guard. But this also caused her to feel stressed whenever she thought about the event. She waited to RSVP until the last minute, and as is typically the case, she landed exactly where she began—choosing to go. She compared her mental process to feeling like she's on a treadmill, working really hard but not getting anywhere new.

Overthinking made Annabelle feel exhausted. She also explained that even though she was functioning well on the outside, she had a lot going on internally without others knowing, which sometimes made her feel lonely. Her mental rituals created a sense of pressure and tension that often led her to engage in other kinds of avoidance behaviors, like those of the Pulsive (e.g., skin picking) and the Otherer (e.g., asking others for input in hopes it would help crystallize the "right" answer).

Annabelle is the Thinker. The Thinker is the person who reduces or avoids distress by worrying, ruminating, thinking through (and mentally solving) every possible outcome and over-analyzing every situation or decision. The Thinker is always in their head. They worry and what-if; they plan for the worst-case scenario; they intellectualize; they ruminate about (or go over and over) past conversations, experiences, or social media posts; and they plan ahead for future conversations. These cognitive strategies give a sense of preparation and problem-solving as well as a greater sense of control and certainty. But they also result in experiencing the pain of every what-if (versus just the pain of one actual outcome) and can limit the Thinker's ability to be truly present. Some Thinkers also have high avoidance tendencies in other domains. As my Hider husband with Thinker tendencies put it, "My overthinking leads me to hide." Annabelle described overthinking leading to Pulsive and Otherer behaviors.

Two of these strategies are more active forms of avoidance (the Doer and the Pulsive), two are more passive (the Hider and the Otherer), and one (the Thinker) is a combination of active and passive.

Active / Do	Passive / Step Back
Doer	Hider
Pulsive	Otherer
Thinker	

Each provides some benefit—they work, or we wouldn't use them—but all come at a cost, ultimately resulting in greater distress and need to avoid and often taking us away from what we value most. You can identify your own primary avoidance strategy by taking the quiz at www.jillstoddard.com/quizzes.

Awareness of avoidance is a necessary first step to change; welcoming discomfort is the next.

The Recap: What to Know
- Avoidance strategies can be categorized into five main sorts: the Doer, the Hider, the Pulsive, the Otherer, and the Thinker.
- You likely engage in strategies across the five sorts but have one you engage in most consistently.

The Work: What to Do
- Take the quiz at www.jillstoddard.com/quizzes to identify your main avoidance type.

Chapter 11

Getting Comfortable Being Uncomfortable

You have to leave the city of your comfort and go into the wilderness of your intuition. . . . What you'll discover will be wonderful. What you'll discover will be yourself.

—*Alan Alda*

In their book *Life Lessons: Two Experts on Death and Dying Teach Us About the Mysteries of Life and Living*, Elisabeth Kübler-Ross and David Kessler begin with the story of Stephanie.[1] Stephanie was driving in the notoriously terrible Southern California traffic from Los Angeles to Palm Springs for a girls' weekend getaway. When the cars in front of her came to a stop, she stopped as well. She glanced in her rearview mirror, only to find the car behind her accelerating with no signs of slowing. Stephanie knew she was about to get slammed, and at the speed the other driver was approaching, she might not make it out alive. She closed her eyes, released her clenched hands from the steering wheel, and let go. Miraculously, despite being hit at full speed, Stephanie emerged unharmed. Her car, the car in front of her, and the car that hit her from behind were demolished, but she was not.

Stephanie survived because she surrendered. Had her body remained tense, hands gripping the steering wheel, she likely would have incurred severe injuries. *It was only in letting go of her resistance and allowing what was to come that she walked away unharmed.* Emotionally, Stephanie realized she had been living her life as if she had a death grip on its steering wheel. The car accident helped her realize she would be better off if she treated her life more like a feather she could hold in her open palm.

This is how I want you to treat your internal experiences—as if you can hold them like a feather in your hand, letting go of your death-grip attempts to control them. Stephanie allowed herself to feel fear, rather than tensing against it. This accepting relationship set her free.

In chapters 9 and 10 we identified your patterns of EA. Now it is time to set you free by teaching you skills to let go of the struggle to control unwanted feelings and develop a new relationship with them. This will mean feelings will no longer serve as obstacles to values-based choices.

THE ANTIDOTE TO STRUGGLE

If control is the problem, letting go is the answer. This is what the *A* in ACT stands for: acceptance. Acceptance doesn't mean liking or wanting an experience; nor does it mean giving up or giving in. Acceptance simply means that we are allowing something to be present that's already there anyway. When we accept internal experiences, we open and allow them to be as they are, no matter how weak or strong, comfortable or uncomfortable. Struggling to control feelings gives them more power, makes them stickier. Pain is part of being human. Resisting pain creates greater suffering and often moves us farther from our values. When we give up resistance, we reduce suffering.

Think of it like using a Hula-Hoop. Most of us can get a Hula-Hoop to circle our waist a few times before it drops. Some people, like circus performers, can Hula-Hoop for ages, even adding additional hoops to their waist, arms, and maybe even one leg. But in every case, the Hula-Hoop eventually drops, or the circus performer adds so many hoops that they are now restricted and no longer able to see or move. Similarly, attempting to control or suppress the feelings you don't want to have may seem doable some of the time. But eventually your ability to keep that up declines. Or you might become so preoccupied with managing your feelings, you can no longer see or do anything else. You're stuck. What if, instead, you left the Hula-Hoop performance under the big top? Dropped the struggle and walked away from all that effort. Like Stephanie, you let go. You surrender. You *accept*.

Research supports the benefits of acceptance. For example, in one study of pain tolerance, research participants were asked to submerge their hands in ice-cold water. Prior to the cold-water exposure, they were divided into three groups. The first group (suppression) was asked to suppress any pain-related emotions, thoughts, and sensations. The second group (acceptance) was asked to accept, observe, and not control pain-related sensations, emotions, and thoughts. The third group (spontaneous coping / control group) was presented with pain education and instructed to use the information to cope with pain. Participants in the acceptance group reported lower pain and distress levels and greater tolerance levels than the other two groups.[2]

Other research has repeated similar findings related to tinnitus (chronic ringing in the ear),[3] chronic pain,[4] panic,[5] and more.

Of course, this is easier said than done, but there are many ways to practice building your acceptance muscles. You can start with easy, playful practices, then move on to more-challenging exercises. We'll explore some of these here.

Using the Breath to Accept Discomfort

Before we jump into our active acceptance exercises, let's pause to discuss what acceptance actually looks like when we're practicing it. I've had several clients tell me they understand the concept of acceptance in theory but not what they're supposed to *do* when they're practicing acceptance. The most effective way I have found to harness acceptance is by using the breath as a vehicle to open and allow discomfort and let go of resistance.

Right now, breathe naturally and observe your body as you breathe. Notice how with each inhale your chest and belly expand, and with each exhale they contract. Now find a spot in your body where you're holding some tension or discomfort. As you inhale, use your breath to open and expand around that tension or discomfort. As you exhale, let go of resistance. Importantly, letting go of resistance does not mean letting go of the tension or discomfort. It means letting go of the need to *control* the tension or discomfort. After a few breaths, I like to incorporate encouraging or instructive words to myself. Here is an example of what that might look like:

Inhale... *Open and expand.*
Exhale... *Let go of resistance.*
Inhale... *Allow.*
Exhale... *Surrender.*
Inhale... *This is here now.*
Exhale... *Let go.*

Inhale... *I have space for this.*

Exhale... *There's nothing that needs to be done here.*

Inhale... *Make space.*

Exhale... While reciting the words above, also drop your shoulders, smooth your face, separate your teeth, unclench your hands—not as a way to force relaxation but to let go of the resistance we hold in our bodies.

At first, you will probably need to close your eyes and really focus on using your breath to create space for your internal experiences, while letting go of resistance. After you've gotten some practice, you will be able to practice with your eyes open, even while focusing on other things, like driving or getting through a challenging interpersonal interaction.

WILLING DISCOMFORT

The key to building acceptance is a willingness to feel uncomfortable. There are many types of stimuli that likely make you feel uncomfortable. Things you prefer not to look at, sounds you prefer not to hear, smells you find offensive, and tastes or textures you consider disgusting. We are going to use these turnoffs to build your acceptance muscles, and you can use your breath to make space for your discomfort while letting go of resistance.

Remember, pain × resistance = suffering. Pain is a given, but we can turn off the resistance to turn down the suffering.

Throughout your day, your brain, eyes, ears, nose, mouth, and skin process many stimuli. When you see something beautiful, like a sunset or rainbow, you probably stop to take it in. When you hear something neutral, like road noise or a computer fan, you may take little notice. When you smell something unappealing, like vomit, you likely plug your nose and do your best to escape the smell.

When we're building psychological flexibility through acceptance, we're becoming more conscious in choosing how we respond when sensations arise. This means we're turning down our autopilot reactions, which would be to avoid or escape internal experiences we find unpleasant. Is there value in accepting the smell of vomit? In the absence of context, not necessarily. And this is not a "no pain, no gain" practice. But what if a loved one gets sick and you need or want to be able to care for them? Being able to be present with the feeling of disgust will allow you to more fully do so. And as you'll see through experience (not just because I'm saying it is so), your suffering in the presence of aversive feelings will decrease the more you open and allow the feelings to just be as they are.

The following practices will allow you to change your relationship with your internal experiences. Doing so will give you the freedom to choose from a greater repertoire of behaviors, unrestrained by an unwillingness to be uncomfortable. And that will allow you to more freely choose values. As you engage in the following practices, pay special attention to your *urges* to avoid. *These* are the feelings we most often react to on autopilot when we choose the comfort zone over workable behavior.

Building Your Visual Acceptance Muscle

To begin, choose a visual stimulus you find appealing. You can do this in your home, out in nature, or on your computer (e.g., by using YouTube or Google Images). Something like a flower, a painting, a pet, or a photograph. Spend a few minutes looking at this stimulus mindfully. Focus on the colors, textures, shape, and overall qualities of the object. Notice how you feel.

Next choose a visual stimulus you find unappealing. Challenge yourself here. Choose something that would rate at least 5 out of 10 on your dislike scale. Perhaps images of snakes, spiders, or my favorite (she said sarcastically), feet. Look at the stimulus the way you normally would, allowing yourself to resist. Maybe you notice your muscles tense, your eyes squint, or your head turn away. Pay attention to how you feel and what you do when you look at something unpleasant. Try not to feel what you feel. Rate your experience of discomfort, resistance, and suffering on a scale of 0–10. If you're not sure how to rate suffering, think of it like distress about your discomfort or the tension that comes with resistance and the feelings you have if resistance fails. For example, when I look at big ugly man feet with long dirty toenails, my discomfort is an 8 out of 10. I do everything in my power to avoid my experience (scrunch up my face, tense up my body, say "Ew, gross, WTF!" and look away if possible, trying to force the memory of the image out of my mind), so my resistance is a 9. I hate how uncomfortable I feel and that my resistance isn't making me feel better (because once I see it, I can't unsee it no matter how hard I try), so my suffering is a 9.

Use the table below to record your own experience.

Visual Stimulus	Discomfort 0-10	Resistance 0-10	Suffering 0-10	Observations
Feet	8	9	9	Tightness in my throat, chest, and belly, squinting, scrunching up face, grunting, trying not to look away but really wanting to look away

After you've looked at the thing that makes you uncomfortable in the way you normally would, likely with resistance, practice looking at it differently. Drop your shoulders; let your face smooth out. Notice the colors, textures, and other qualities without judgment. Use your breath to open and expand around the sensations created by looking at this unappealing stimulus. Stay with it. Breathe, and allow your internal experiences to just be. Maybe even look at the images and your sensations with curiosity. In other words, drop your resistance and practice acceptance. Rate your discomfort, resistance, and suffering on a scale of 0–10, and record your experience using the table below.

Visual Stimulus	Discomfort 0-10	Resistance 0-10	Suffering 0-10	Observations
Feet	5	2	2	Open, relaxed, curious, still don't like the image, but less tension and distress, was able to look longer

Notice how your experience differs when you resist versus accept. Did your discomfort and suffering ratings change? Did your willingness to stay with it change? Your behavior?

Building Your Auditory Acceptance Muscle

I absolutely love the sound of my dog snoring. He's a French bulldog, so sometimes he snores even when he's not sleeping. It's adorable and hilarious, and it makes me want to kiss his little smoosh face. But human mouth sounds? No thank you. If I had a dime for every time I have snapped at my husband or daughter for chewing their nails, I'd have the world's largest dime collection. Often, my snapping at them also involves a reflexive smack on the arm that startles them and is not very kind. So I've started practicing acceptance toward Billy's and Scarlett's mouth sounds. What sounds do you enjoy, and how do they make you feel? Which ones make you want to jump out of your own skin? Let's practice building acceptance toward the latter ones.

Start with a sound or sounds you find pleasant. Maybe a piece of music, birds chirping, or waves crashing. Spend a few minutes listening to the sound mindfully. Focus on the volume, pitch, timbre, and overall qualities of the sounds. Let go of judgments and notice how you feel.

Next, choose an auditory stimulus you find unappealing. Remember to challenge yourself, choosing something that would rate at least 5 out of 10 on your dislike scale. This could be a baby crying, nails on a chalkboard (YouTube is great for this, if you don't have access to an actual chalkboard), or music by an artist you don't like or in a genre you can't stand. Listen as you normally would, resistance and all. Notice what you do with your body and how you feel (try to avoid assault if the noise is coming from a person or animal). Rate your experience of discomfort, resistance, and suffering on a 10-point scale when you resist, and record it in the table below.

Auditory Stimulus	Discomfort 0–10	Resistance 0–10	Suffering 0–10	Observations
Song by the Cars	6	7	7	Feeling of disgust and annoyance, longing for it to end, my ears hurt

Now listen with an accepting ear. If you're listening to music, notice each instrument separately. Focus on the qualities of the sounds with curiosity rather than judgment. Use your breath as a vehicle to allow yourself to feel whatever arises. Rate your experience of discomfort, resistance, and suffering on a 10-point scale when you accept, and record it in the table below.

Auditory Stimulus	Discomfort 0–10	Resistance 0–10	Suffering 0–10	Observations
Song by the Cars	3	1	1	Noticed interesting instruments I wasn't aware of before, was able to listen until the end without urgency, liked the harmonies

Building Your Olfactory Acceptance Muscle

Call me crazy, but I absolutely love the smell of gasoline. And bug spray. And campfires. Last year, I bought an electric car. Never needing to get gas is quite a convenience, but I do miss that smell. Gin, on the other hand, makes me physically gag. Of course, there's a reason, but that's a story for another book. Many household and commercial cleaners smell exactly like gin, so I can't always avoid the scent. What's the alternative? Acceptance. Which smells do you love? Which do you hate? Let's practice accepting the ones you'd rather avoid.

First, choose a smell you find appealing. Perhaps your puppy's breath, a flower, your partner's cologne, or the top of a baby's head. Spend a few minutes smelling this stimulus mindfully. Focus on the overall qualities of the scent. Let go of judgments, and notice how you feel.

Next, choose an odor you find unappealing. Again, challenge yourself. Choose something that would rate at least 5 out of 10 on your dislike scale. Perhaps a stinky cheese, your partner's feet at the end of the day, or the litter box when it needs to be cleaned. Smell the stimulus the way you normally would, allowing yourself to resist. Maybe you notice you scrunch up your nose or vocalize your disgust. Pay attention to how you feel and what you do when you smell something unpleasant. Rate your experience of discomfort, resistance, and suffering on a scale of 0–10, and record it in the table below.

Olfactory Stimulus	Discomfort 0-10	Resistance 0-10	Suffering 0-10	Observations
Billy's feet	8	10	8	Total disgust, vocalization, questioning what's wrong, face scrunched up, moved face away and gave up instantly

After you've smelled it the way you normally would, likely with resistance, practice smelling it differently. Unwrinkle your nose. Notice the qualities without judgment. Use your breath to open and expand around the sensations created by smelling this unappealing odor. Stay with it. Breathe, and allow your internal experiences to just be. Maybe even treat the odor with curiosity. In other words, drop your resistance and practice acceptance. Rate your discomfort, resistance, and suffering on a scale of 0–10, and record it below.

Olfactory Stimulus	Discomfort 0-10	Resistance 0-10	Suffering 0-10	Observations
Billy's feet	5	3	3	Still don't like it at all but could stay with it and even got curious about the different details of the odor. Actually found his Fred Flintstone feet to be kind of cute.

Notice how your experience differs when you resist versus accept. Did your discomfort and suffering ratings change? Did your willingness to stay with it change? Your behavior?

Building Your Gustatory Acceptance Muscle (the BeanBoozled Challenge)

In late February of 2020, my mischievous son decided he needed to know what would happen if he put a pebble in his ear canal. At the advice of his pediatrician, we brought him to urgent care. In February. Of 2020. About a week later, everything William put in his mouth was declared *"Dithguthting!"* Thankfully, his COVID-induced loss of taste and smell was temporary (and his illness mild), but he remains a very picky eater to this day. Of course, we all have likes and dislikes when it comes to food and drink. If you're getting your nutritional needs met, there's no need to force yourself to eat foods you dislike. But it's a great way to practice building your acceptance muscle. In fact, it's my favorite way.

As before, to begin, choose something edible you enjoy eating. Spend a few minutes enjoying this food mindfully. Focus on the taste and texture and overall qualities of the food. Let go of judgments, and notice how you feel.

Next, choose a food you find unappealing. I like to do this one with my clients, using BeanBoozled jelly beans. You can buy these online, and they're inexpensive. The jelly beans come in a variety of colors and flavors. The peach-colored bean with red speckles might be strawberry banana smoothie...or it might be dead fish. The white one with multicolored spots might be birthday cake... or it might be dirty dishwater. If you don't want to purchase the jelly beans, you can do this with any food you don't care for. Taste the food the way you normally would, allowing yourself to resist. If you take the BeanBoozled challenge, pop one in your mouth, and notice the anticipation and maybe curiosity coupled with dread. When you bite into the bean and the flavor registers, notice relief when you get a "good" flavor; notice the strong urge to spit out the "bad" flavor. Go ahead and spit it out the first time around as you normally would. Pay attention to how you feel and what you do when you taste something unpleasant. Rate your experience of discomfort, resistance, and suffering on a scale of 0–10, and record it below.

Gustatory Stimulus	Discomfort 0-10	Resistance 0-10	Suffering 0-10	Observations
BeanBoozled jelly bean	7	10	8	Dread, then as soon as the dead fish taste registered, crinkled up face, felt and vocalized disgust, and spit out the bean

After you've eaten the item the way you normally would, likely with resistance, practice tasting it differently. Notice the flavors, textures, and other qualities without judgment. Use your breath to open and expand around the sensations created by tasting unappealing food. Stay with it. Breathe, and allow your internal experiences to just be. If you take the BeanBoozled challenge, practice an open, curious, willing stance toward whatever flavor you get, knowing they're all just jelly beans. In other words, drop your resistance and practice acceptance. Rate your discomfort, resistance, and suffering on a scale of 0–10, and record it below.

Gustatory Stimulus	Discomfort 0–10	Resistance 0–10	Suffering 0–10	Observations
BeanBoozled jelly bean	0	0	0	Open, curious, interested, relieved when buttered popcorn registered and it wasn't rotten egg!

Notice how your experience differs when you resist versus accept. Did your discomfort and suffering ratings change? Did your willingness to stay with it change? Your behavior?

Building Your Tactile Acceptance Muscle

I like the cash in my wallet to face the same way, in denominational order. I like the seams of my to-go coffee cup to line up with the seams of the heat-protective cuff. I always curl the left side of my hair before the right. And I always, always wear my watch on my left wrist. If the cash is messy, the cup seams are misaligned, my hair is styled out of order, or my watch is worn on the other hand, I feel uncomfortable. Like it's just wrong. Feeling wrong is a right way to practice acceptance.

For this exercise, you can choose to practice with anything you do in a routine way—brushing your teeth, shaving, showering, getting dressed, tying your shoes, doing dishes or laundry, etc. You can also choose anything that involves a feeling on your skin—wearing jewelry, eyeglasses, or earbuds. With each of these, start by just doing what you normally do. Put your pants on one leg at a time as always. If you wear a ring on your left middle finger, do that. Notice how it feels. Notice that you usually don't even notice!

Now mix it up. Do it in a funny-feeling way. Wear your ring on the wrong finger. Brush your teeth with your nondominant hand. Take a shower in a different order (e.g., soap before shampoo). Put your glasses on upside down or your earbuds in the wrong ears. Have fun with it—be playful! Pay attention to how you feel and what you do when something feels like it's just not right. Notice the urge to go back to the comfortable way. Start by allowing yourself to resist, and go back to the good-feeling way as soon as the desire strikes you. Rate your experience of discomfort, resistance, and suffering on a scale of 0–10, and record it in the table provided.

Tactile Stimulus	Discomfort 0–10	Resistance 0–10	Suffering 0–10	Observations
Folding my hands the "wrong" way	4	10	4	Felt funny and distressing, had an immediate urge to switch it out, so I stopped and did it the "right" way right away

Now practice allowing the funny-feeling way. Simply notice your experience. Use your breath to open and expand around the sensations. Stay with it. Breathe, and allow your internal experiences to just be. Maybe even look at your urges with curiosity. In other words, drop your resistance and practice acceptance. Rate your discomfort, resistance, and suffering on a scale of 0–10, and record it below.

Tactile Stimulus	Discomfort 0-10	Resistance 0-10	Suffering 0-10	Observations
Folding my hands the "wrong" way	2	0	0	Allowed hands to stay in that position and simply observed and allowed. Still felt funny, but this dissipated with time and there was no distress.

Notice how your experience differs when you resist versus accept. Did your discomfort and suffering ratings change? Did your willingness to stay with it change? Your behavior?

These practices may seem silly and unrelated to imposterism. But if I said, "Just accept your self-doubt and anxiety and live full-size!" you'd be as successful as if I said, "Just go run a marathon!" when you'd never trained a day in your life. Practicing acceptance of discomfort in these playful, benign ways is how you train. You can work your way up from brushing your teeth the funny-feeling way to accepting anxiety, self-doubt, insecurity, dread, anger, envy, guilt, shame, and all the other uncomfortable feelings we work so hard to avoid. Trust me—if you can get comfortable being uncomfortable, you will unlock an immense amount of freedom in your life. Share your playful practices on social media, tag me, and use the hashtag #imposternomore.

Building Your Emotional Acceptance Muscles

We're not done yet. Your five-senses practices were only the beginning. Now it's time to practice with the heavyweights—your emotions. As we've talked about in the last two chapters, when you look to the places you are not living in line with your values, avoidance of uncomfortable emotions is likely a big part of the reason why. So let's practice doing things differently.

Just like you did in the five-senses exercises above, start with a feeling you enjoy. Maybe watch a sitcom or stand-up comedy show that makes you laugh, or ride a roller coaster if you love that sort of thing (I do!). Whatever you choose to do, notice how it makes you feel and how you respond to emotions you enjoy experiencing.

Now choose a stimulus that will evoke feelings that are challenging for you. This could be watching sad YouTube movie clips, like scenes from *My Girl*, *Beaches*, or *Terms of Endearment*. My absolute favorite is the gut-wrenching *Marley & Me* montage of Marley's final moments. You could also watch scary movie clips, especially the ones with jump scares, or go on a roller coaster if you absolutely hate those sorts of things. Maybe you struggle with jealousy and can comb through some LinkedIn profiles of professionals who you see as more successful than you. For anger, find a politician you dislike, and listen to one of their speeches. There is no shortage of options. If you can't come up with one, reach out to me, and I'll try to help you find a perfect fit.

The first time you engage with the emotionally evocative stimulus, allow yourself to resist, and notice the experience. Rate your discomfort, resistance, and suffering on a scale of 0–10, and record it in the table below.

Emotional Stimulus	Discomfort 0–10	Resistance 0–10	Suffering 0–10	Observations
Marley & Me	9	10	9	Instant crying but tried to stuff it down; tight chest, throat, and belly; turned it off after thirty seconds

Then keep going while practicing acceptance. You should be getting pretty good at this by now after your five-senses practices. Note that getting pretty good at it does not necessarily mean feeling better or more comfortable! It means you're building your willingness to be *un*comfortable. Rate your experience in the table below.

Emotional Stimulus	Discomfort 0–10	Resistance 0–10	Suffering 0–10	Observations
Marley & Me	5	0	0	Breathing deeply, open, interested, allowing, focusing on the love and connection

Notice how your experience differs when you resist versus accept. Did your discomfort and suffering ratings change? Did your willingness to stay with it change? Your behavior?

Now take these practices into your life. Notice when you're resisting something uncomfortable, and stop clenching the steering wheel. Hold the experience in your open palm like a feather. Notice and allow your feelings, using your breath, without doing anything to control or suppress them. Then choose to persist or pivot in your behavior based on values.

This creates a new context where internal experiences no longer act as obstacles to values-based choices. We think and feel and do what matters irrespective of how compelling a thought seems or how uncomfortable a feeling may be. In other words, we FLEX:

F: feel feelings
L: let thoughts pass
EX: execute valued behavior

Learning to accept discomfort is an ongoing, lifelong process. You will never wake up one morning saying, "Aha, I have arrived! I have mastered acceptance! Check it off the list and move on to the next!" Acceptance is something you will need to return to each and every day. It will get easier the more you practice, but it is a process, not an end point.

Changing your relationship with thoughts and to feelings where you observe thoughts without getting hooked, as well as allow feelings without resistance, is the key to psychological flexibility.

WHAT ARE YOU WILLING TO FEEL?

Joy and pain are often two sides of the same coin. To love is to risk loss. To succeed is to risk failure. To create is to risk critique. To truly have a full-size life, you must be willing to carry both the feelings that you enjoy as well as those that are more difficult to experience. What are you willing to feel to have the life you want? Using my example below as a model, write down one or two of your own in the table provided.

What I want to do	How I might feel if I do it	How I will feel if I don't
Create a new, live two-day workshop	Terrified! What if people hate it and feel like they wasted their money? What if it doesn't help anyone? What if I fail? But maybe also proud of myself for trying.	Disappointed that I didn't try when it's really important to me. Angry that I let my self-doubt decide. Cowardly for letting my feelings get in the way.

Consider writing your "What I want to do" on an index card or a small piece of paper with your "How I might feel if I do it" on the back side. You can rip that card up or throw it away any time if you want to toss those uncomfortable feelings aside. But doing so also means throwing away your dreams.

Even when you live your values, you won't necessarily feel better! Going after what you want means being willing to take risks and be vulnerable. This will likely feel more uncomfortable...at first. But with that discomfort also comes pride, vitality, purpose, meaning, and feeling more alive. It's worth it. And you can do it. As you'll learn in part III, doing it with community, compassion, and a culture shift is important.

The Recap: What to Know

- If attempting to control how you feel is the problem, acceptance is the solution.
- Acceptance does not mean liking, wanting, giving up, or giving in. It means allowing what is already here.
- You can practice acceptance using your five senses, changing your routine, and evoking emotions.
- Acceptance is an ongoing process, not an end point.
- FLEX: feel feelings, let thoughts pass, execute valued behavior.
- Pain and joy are two sides of the same coin; you must be willing to experience one to get the other.

The Work: What to Do

- Practice acceptance using your senses and routines and by stimulating challenging emotions. Let your breath be your vehicle.
- Consider what you want and what you must be willing to feel to get it. Practice acceptance of those emotions.

Part III

LIVING FULL-SIZE
(NOT FUN-SIZE)

Chapter 12

Together We Can: Connecting with Community and Changing the World

Alone we can do so little; together we can do so much.

—Helen Keller

When I wrote *The Big Book of ACT Metaphors,* my publisher encouraged me to attend the annual conference of the Association for Contextual Behavioral Science (ACBS). They wanted my coauthor and me to do a book signing with the attendees, who were the intended audience for our book. I had just given birth to my son three months earlier. I was torn about leaving him and felt guilty asking my husband to single-parent a newborn and a two-year-old. I also wasn't thrilled at the prospect of lugging a breast pump from San Diego to Minneapolis. But I wanted my book to succeed, so I decided to compromise and attend two of the six conference days.

During registration, signs indicated where to line up based on the first letter of your last name. One sign read "F–K (thank your mind for that thought)." Between that, seeing ACT bigwigs in casual clothes, wearing badge ribbons with jokes on them, and the Follies—a Saturday-night performance of skits, songs, and stand-up comedy themed around contextual behavioral science—I was sold. I knew I had found my professional home.

After a couple of years, I wanted to become a more active member of the association, to contribute to the organization that had given me so much. I had already been serving on the awards committee and had joined the women's special interest group. But I wanted to do something bigger and with more reach. I decided to run for a seat on the board. Despite feeling insecure and imposter-y, I nominated myself, completed the requisite bios and platform statements, and waited to hear what would come next. I learned that a committee was tasked with vetting all the nominees and choosing two candidates to run from the pool. I was not selected for the ballot.

The following year, when the call for board nominations came again, my inner critic and imposter voice reminded me of my failure the previous year. Sheila warned me not to make a fool of myself by attempting to run again. She told me I wasn't well known or productive enough to be considered. And I believed her.

Then several colleagues from the women's special interest group urged me on. They told me I was enough—that the board would be lucky to have me. I didn't believe it myself and worried they were just being nice, but I took a leap of faith that maybe they really meant it. Maybe they believed in me, and maybe they even saw something in me that I couldn't see in myself.

The support and encouragement from my community gave me the courage to try again. This time I was selected for the ballot and won the election. During my tenure as member-at-large, I was nominated to run for secretary/treasurer and was elected to that position as well.

When I struggled to act psychologically flexible in the face of potential failure and humiliation, I was able to lean on my community. I was better able to embody the values of courage and persistence with their support. And I knew if I failed again, I would be OK because they would have my back.

Humans crave connection, and the benefit of community—a feeling of fellowship with others as a result of sharing common attitudes, interests, and goals—is clear. In education, teachers demonstrate greater efficacy, morale, satisfaction, and attendance when they work in a school that prioritizes community.[1] When a community of people dances together in synchrony, they experience a strong sense of connection and exhibit greater trust, cooperation, and pain tolerance.[2] Kids and teens with healthy peer communities are less likely to develop substance use problems as adults.[3] And individuals who feel a strong sense of group belonging tend to be more generous and care about the outcomes of others.[4] In contrast, loneliness—an emotional state of feeling disconnected from others—is as deadly as cigarette smoking. One meta-analysis of sixteen longitudinal studies demonstrated that poor social connections put people at risk for cardiovascular disease and robustly predicted morbidity and mortality.[5]

When it comes to cultivating a full-size professional life, consider how building a community might help you move forward when self-doubt and imposterism rear their ugly heads. I posed the following questions on Twitter, itself a type of community: "How has COMMUNITY helped you move forward professionally during times of self-doubt or imposterism? In what ways have you cultivated community?" Here are some of the answers I received:

- "I reached out to a few brilliant writers to start a monthly mastermind group."
  —@DrEmilyEdlynn (Lucky for me, I happen to be one of those writers, and our new mastermind group starts this week!)
- "A community of amazing writer friends has helped! But also, I try to remind myself that the feedback I receive from the community about my work is likely more accurate than my skewed perception of self (due to imposterism)."
  —@TherapistTamara
- "Oh, wow. This is like what VMUG is all about. The community we've cultivated has been amazing for me and others. Reach out if you'd like some details."
  —@steveathanas
- "Pretty sure that if [others in my community] hadn't pointed to me and said 'you're a VMUG leader now,' I'm not sure I'd be where I am now, or as *comfortable.*"
  —@RichardKenyan

I reached out to Steve Athanas to ask more about the VMUG (VMware User Group) community, as he suggested. VMUG is an online user group for technology professionals who use a software product called VMware. Steve explained that "the community around VMUG is so much more than just one company's product." He noted that the VMUG members are there for each other and support each other through the trials and tribulations of a tech career. As a result of their interactive online community, Steve has witnessed multiple members get promotions they didn't think they were qualified for, pass certification exams they "knew" they would fail, and present in front of audiences they were convinced they never could. The members of the VMUG community help each other realize they are more talented than they give themselves credit for, and they share their talents with the community to help one another creatively solve big problems in their technology positions.

When I spoke to bestselling author Eve Rodsky about the role of community in making values-based changes, she identified two important benefits to community. First, community helps us get past the stage of the "delicate dream." Eve recounted the story of Sandy Zimmerman, a woman featured in her book *Find Your Unicorn Space: Reclaim Your Creative Life in a Too-Busy World*.[6] Sandy was the first and oldest mother to complete the American Ninja Warrior (ANW) obstacle course. For Sandy, *sharing* her ANW dream with supportive others (what Eve calls *connection* in *Find Your Unicorn Space*) helped her push past self-doubt; it also helped hold her accountable, so she was less likely to back out when imposter thoughts threatened to derail her.

Eve said the second benefit to community is that having accountability partners helps combat marginalization. If you can share experiences with others who look like you and have had similar life experiences, you will know you're not alone, feel validated, and feel less like an imposter. This was true for Eve herself when her original book proposal for *Fair Play* was rejected. Eve created her Fair Play system for gender equality based on the shared experiences of hundreds of working moms who were at the end of their ropes, just like Eve. When Eve's proposal was rejected and she experienced self-doubt, she remembered the women she was fighting for—she didn't want to let them down, so she kept going. She also noted it was easier for her to stand up for something knowing she wasn't alone. Eve is now a two-time best-selling author who has made dozens of high-profile media appearances and even produced a *Fair Play* documentary with Reese Witherspoon and Hello Sunshine. She credits much of her success to the role of community.

HOW TO CULTIVATE COMMUNITY

The concept of building community may feel daunting, but there are so many ways to go about doing it. One way is to simply build on the connections you already have. Tracy, with whom I've been friends since we were dormmates in college, is a former nurse and military spouse who recently returned to full-time work. She asked to meet up for lunch so she could pick my brain about how to best juggle her schedule. I loved that she thought to ask me about this specific area because she sees it as something I have figured out how to do well. She reached out to other friends for advice on their strengths as well. When my friend and colleague Brian was writing his first book, he reached out to me regularly to ask for book-writing and publishing advice. I, in turn, asked if he would help me with an example for this book (you may remember Brian's self-critical thoughts from chapter 8). Giving and receiving support to and from one another, especially when we're engaged in solitary endeavors like writing, gives both of us a sense of community. In your first bid to cultivate a professional community, you can take a page from Tracy's and Brian's books and reach out to friends or colleagues for advice in their areas of strength—if they're local, you might offer to treat them to lunch or coffee so you can chat about your goals, questions, or struggles without feeling like you're taking advantage of their precious time for free.

In addition to tapping your current connections, you can build new connections in myriad ways:

- **Join a professional association.** Look for one whose members share your passions, values, or goals. If the association is large, consider joining a committee, special interest group, or local chapter to give you more opportunities to interact with members.
- **Join or create a consultation or mastermind group.** These are usually small groups of people with similar professions or goals. These groups often discuss the current state of their work lives, goals for their futures, and ideas for how to achieve those goals and overcome obstacles. They also offer emotional support and encouragement.
- **Collaborate.** Instead of writing an article, book, or chapter alone, find a coauthor. Instead of starting a solo podcast, see if you can find a partner who shares a passion for the topic. You might even offer to join someone who is already writing a column or hosting a podcast you love. They may have more work than they can handle and may be craving community too. Writing a research grant? Ask another lab to join forces. Giving a talk? Seek out a co-presenter. In some cases, collaborating might mean having to divide revenue, but it also might mean sharing resources, which can save money too.
- **Find or become a mentor.** Even a community of just two people can offer benefits! Having a mentor can help steer you in valued directions and boost your confidence. When I talked with Marie Schiller, former VP of Eli Lilly and Company and current CEO and cofounder of Chronicles Health,

she credited her mentors with giving her the confidence to climb the ranks when she felt like a fraud. They believed in her and had her back even when she made costly errors. Now, as a mentor herself, she tries to send the message "You belong, you matter, and what you do is valued." Being a mentor helps lift others up, but it can also remind *you* how much you know and have to offer, which is a great confidence booster. Not to mention giving to others boosts happiness.[7]

- **Find a podcast community.** There are podcasts for every interest. Most podcasts have social media accounts where you can interact with the hosts or other listeners. Some offer classes or book clubs. Some invite you to reach out with questions they might use on air. I donate twenty-five dollars per month through Patreon to one of my favorite podcasts, *Writing Class Radio*. In exchange, I get to attend a high-value weekly critique group with the hosts and other listeners. Not only has it provided a sense of community, but it has greatly improved my writing! My podcast, *Psychologists Off the Clock*, holds a free monthly book club where you can nerd out about psychology books with our team and other listeners. You might also consider starting your own podcast with colleagues who share your passions. Even if your podcast has a small following, it can be a great way to connect with like-minded guests, listeners, or cohosts.

- **Take a course.** Whether virtual or in person, workshops and classes are a great way to meet people with similar interests and goals—they want to learn the same stuff you do! Many of these involve learning or practicing with smaller breakout groups. Consider asking your fellow learners to continue meeting with you after the course ends to talk about how you're implementing what you've learned, obstacles you've encountered, and ideas for moving forward. I wrote my last book after a breakout group from an ACT workshop turned into a regular writing group.

- **Find a meetup.** Meetup groups exist for virtually any interest. Want to get together with other people in your city who have poodles, like to Rollerblade, or drink loose-leaf tea? I guarantee there's a meetup for it. You can find or create these online, then decide whether and when you'd like to meet up in person.

- **Find your people on social media.** At times, social media can be a time-sucking curse and an avoidance strategy. But it can also be a place you can connect with other professionals. On Twitter, I interact with other writers using the hashtags #writingcommunity and #amwriting, and with other therapists using the hashtags #therapisttwitter and #psychtwitter. The key is to actually interact, not just scroll. I have landed podcast guests, stayed in contact with podcast guests, and been invited to be on podcasts and in a mastermind group because of my activity on Twitter and Instagram.

- **Create an office community.** You don't have to go outside your work environment to build community; you can do so right in your own office. Maybe you plan a Super Bowl pool or NCAA tournament brackets. Gambling not allowed? Try a monthly book club, happy hour, or lunch outing where you rotate who chooses the restaurant.

It's important to be clear on and realistic about what you hope to get out of the community-building strategies you choose. It may be harder to truly connect with those you know only through social media than with those you have in-person or Zoom meetings with. You will also get out only as much as you put in. In her book, *How to Have a Kid and a Life*, Ericka Sóuter talks about the importance of putting in the time when it comes to parents cultivating a community.[8] She cites the research of Jeffrey Hall, a University of Kansas professor who studied the amount of time we need to spend with others to truly forge a bond. For an acquaintance to become a casual friend, you're looking at about fifty hours of quality time together. For that casual friend to become a good friend, plan on ninety hours. To become a very close friend? Two hundred hours of quality time. Of note, Ericka told me texts count! So don't worry if you can't put in face time. As long as the time is quality time, it's the interacting that matters, not the method. Lately, whenever I hear a song that reminds me of someone I care about, I shoot them a text to let them know. I imagine it gives both of us some warm community-building fuzzies. Of course, you may not desire to forge deep personal bonds in your professional circles, but building any community where you feel a sense of camaraderie and support will require your investment. And if you're not sure what you need, test out a couple of the suggestions above and let your experience—and new community!—be your guide. It's generally preferable to learn by doing rather than to wait around until you have it all figured out.

Getting Intimate

When I talked more with Marie Schiller about community, mentorship, imposterism, and success, she highlighted the importance of intimacy even in professional relationships. She suggested one of the best ways to identify mentors or mentees is to be willing to spend time together beyond simply solving problems at work. To build community, she encouraged getting together outside the office and sharing a bit of your nonwork life. Marie identified trust, respect, and care as being critical ingredients to building psychological safety and intimacy. Her advice for gaining the most benefit out of community is to go beyond "just being work acquaintances."

Building relationships outside the office does not have to mean becoming BFFs with your coworkers. And don't let the word *intimacy* scare you. What we're talking about here is creating camaraderie. This might mean axe throwing while you dish about a pain-in-the-butt customer, or texting over the weekend about a great facial, but it doesn't have to mean you share the most intimate details of your painful divorce or childhood trauma. Of course, you *can* do this if it feels safe and appropriate, but really, I'm encouraging a tasteful stretch beyond your work to-do list while still maintaining boundaries to the degree that feels right for you. There's no real formula here—you get to be the judge of what intimacy in the workplace looks like for you.

IF YOU CAN'T SEE IT, CAN YOU STILL BE IT?

In 2004, while watching children's television programs with her daughter, actress Geena Davis noticed that male characters greatly outnumbered female characters. Wishing to promote greater equality in Hollywood, she founded the Geena Davis Institute on Gender in Media, the only global nonprofit research-based organization to work collaboratively with the entertainment industry to create gender balance, foster inclusion, and reduce negative stereotyping in family entertainment media.[9]

Davis also created a community around her movement. She has a social media group, membership plans, events, and tool kits—a plethora of community-oriented resources. She has been recognized for coining the phrase "If she can see it, she can be it" and using the hashtag #seeitbeit to highlight the importance of girls seeing women on screen portraying a variety of professional roles, not just those that promote gender stereotypes. In other words, when girls don't see themselves in leadership, STEM, law enforcement, or other traditionally male-dominated arenas, they are less likely to believe there are seats at those tables available to them. The same can be assumed for BIPOC, LGBTQIA+ folks, immigrants, individuals with disabilities, and other marginalized people.

While the research on imposterism among marginalized individuals leaves many questions unanswered, it stands to reason that when we don't see people who look or identify like us in a certain role, we are more likely to experience imposterism if we dare venture into that role. Callie Womble Edwards, a Black female scholar working in a predominantly white male academy, wrote in her autoethnography investigating imposter syndrome and stereotype threat among professional Black women, "Context plays a vital role in the imposter syndrome as women are looking to others to determine what characteristics make one an authentic academic or professional. In comparing themselves to whom they deem as authentic academics or professionals, women notice differences and begin to feel like counterfeits."[10]

Stereotype Threat

Stereotype threat describes a situation in which an individual is concerned about being judged negatively or treated poorly on the basis of their belongingness to a stereotyped group. Simply being aware of negative stereotypes can actually impair performance and undermine aspirations.[11] With imposterism, we feel as if we do not belong. With stereotype threat, we feel we must prove that we do. It makes sense that these two distinct but related concepts would interact for marginalized individuals.

The real cure for imposterism and stereotype threat would be to end social oppression toward all disenfranchised groups at the organizational and systemic level, and I hope there is a future where this becomes a reality. However, in lieu of waiting for change to trickle down slowly from the top, perhaps we can make changes at the individual level—like grassroots changes—that in large enough numbers will trickle from the bottom up. That may go against the law of gravity, but a handful of really smart people figured out how to get a ninety-thousand-pound hunk of metal to reliably fly high in the sky, so maybe we should try to follow suit. In other words, we can do it, and I think knowledge, practice, psychological flexibility, and community can be our start. Like Margaret Mead is thought to have said, "Never doubt that a small group of thoughtful, committed citizens can change the world. Indeed, it is the only thing that ever has."

I first learned the term *stereotype threat* from Jamil, whom you met in chapter 2 as the Perfectionist Imposter. For him, just knowing about stereotype threat helped him break free of some of his perfectionistic tendencies and imposter fears. And in fact, experiments support this. For example, one study demonstrated that when participants were educated about stereotype threat and reassured that stereotypes are illegitimate, impaired performance on a math test was restored.[12]

Here's what Jamil told me:

I remember learning about this [stereotype threat] from Dr. Claude Steele at Stanford in Psych 101 and I remember thinking, *holy shit, this is exactly how I feel anytime I am called on in class or have to give a presentation or am given a promotion.* I think you captured the sentiment in this sentence about me [written in chapter 2, which I had him review before publishing], 'He worried that mistakes would reflect poorly not only on him but on the Black community as a whole.' After learning that there was such a concept of stereotype threat, it made me feel more okay with maybe sometimes I wouldn't get it perfect, and that it was okay because of the enormous weight/anxiety on my shoulders for my race. So, once I knew that this phenomenon existed, it made it less stress provoking when I was thrust into the spotlight. Less stress meant I could perform better, and then each success built on the previous one until I built up confidence in myself and my abilities to the point that I felt like I belonged or was worthy. I'm not sure where I would be if I didn't learn about that concept in Psych 101, but it definitely made me feel better about not having to ace everything that I ever tried.

My editor for this book is one of very few Black female VPs in the publishing industry, which she described as both "amazing and also a real challenge at alternating moments." When you're one of the first or the few, the bias, discrimination, and ensuing imposterism can be a serious challenge. But you also get to be the one the others see—when they see you, they are more likely to believe they can be like you. Amazing indeed.

In much the same way building community can foster courage and willingness to pursue our dreams amid self-doubt and imposterism, so too can the knowledge that we are working for the greater good. We don't have to wait until we can see it to be it. We can *choose* to be the first or among the few in service of being the one others will ultimately see. It's a form of community that's like taking one for the team. Of course, this is no mean feat and takes a good deal of courage and willingness to step out into the open. But as we say yes to these roles, more people like us will be invited into them. It will create momentum and change.

Consider the US women's national soccer team players Hope Solo, Carli Lloyd, Rebecca Sauerbrunn, Alex Morgan, and Megan Rapinoe, who filed a complaint with the Equal Employment Opportunity Commission against the US Soccer Federation (USSF), citing gender discrimination based on unequal pay. The US women's team had won four World Cup championship titles and four Olympic gold medals, while the US men's team had won zero of each. Yet the men were being paid four times more than the women. In a historic turn of events, the USSF and the two players associations agreed to a deal to provide equal pay to the men's and women's teams. On the heels of this momentous occasion, the National Women's Soccer League (NWSL) announced the formation of the Angel City team, the first-ever women-founded and women-led NWSL team.

As Gandhi taught, If we could change ourselves, the tendencies in the world would also change. Gandhi never promised it would be smooth sailing, that we would feel confident or free from self-doubt, imposterism, or stereotype threat. The more it matters, the harder it will feel.

INFLUENCE IS YOUR SUPERPOWER

If you're on board with trying to change yourself so the world will also change—tackling imposterism by attempting to change organizations or systems—you're going to need some influence. Zoe Chance is a writer, professor, and researcher who teaches the most popular class at the Yale School of Management: Mastering Influence and Persuasion. She wrote an international best-selling book, *Influence Is Your Superpower*.[13] My podcast cohost Yael interviewed her about having influence, and what Chance had to say was both compelling and a little surprising. Here are some of the main takeaways:

1. **Be an empathic listener.** The most powerful way you can influence others is through *empathic listening*. Chance recommended listening for fifteen minutes, then reflecting back what you heard. For example, you might say, "It sounds like you care about X" or "It's important to you to feel Y." Listening and reflecting creates a connection and develops empathy. Interestingly, even if your reflection isn't accurate, the process of listening and reflecting will still be effective in nurturing the relationship and helping the other party feel heard. The speaker will have the opportunity to correct your reflection and will feel grateful and respected because you tried and cared enough to listen even if you didn't totally get it right. Research supports this. One study of heterosexual couples found that empathic *effort* was more important than empathic *accuracy* for relationship satisfaction.[14] Often, when a person feels heard, they will reciprocate by asking what matters to you. Chance emphasized that the act of listening itself is what's influential— you can let go of trying to persuade, and simply listen.

Chance also believes that to be influen*tial* you have to be influen*ceable*. For over a year, I had been trying to persuade my husband to move back to the East Coast from San Diego with zero success. At one point we had a totally unrelated disagreement. Normally, I would have been defensive and stood my ground. But this time, I slowed down, listened, and reflected my understanding of how he was feeling. Billy effectively persuaded me, and I agreed to his request. He told me he had never felt so seen or understood. A few weeks later, he agreed to move back east. These two incidents had nothing to do with one another, but I think Billy was more open to my reasons for wanting to move after he felt heard and was able to influence me during our other disagreement. In both cases, listening to one another influenced us in a powerful way.

2. **Use your human voice.** In-person conversations are more persuasive than emails, texts, or social media posts, even when using the exact same words.[15] When we hear others' voices, we perceive them to be more intelligent, persuasive, and worthy of our empathy. You will be two to three times more likely to get a yes if you make an in-person request than if you ask via email.

3. **Be transparent.** People don't like to feel manipulated, so don't hide your agenda. You can give options—which gives the chooser a sense of control—and still be influential by nudging them in the desired direction. For example, a human resources department might automatically opt employees in to their 401(k) plan because it believes this will be beneficial when they retire. Employees still have the option to opt out, but behavioral science shows that opt-ins are powerful ways to nudge behavior (because most people won't opt out). Similarly, when you give a child two to three options from which they can choose, they will be far more likely to comply than if you tell them what to do. When

people feel like they are being told what to do, they will often do the exact opposite. This is such a common phenomenon that it even has a name: *psychological reactance.*[16]

These three skills also make me think of calling people in versus calling people out. When we get called out, we feel attacked, cornered, bullied, or misunderstood. This leads to defensiveness rather than openness to being influenced. When agendas are transparent and we feel heard and understood—especially when talking directly to another person (versus reading their social media pleas)—we feel like we are being "called in" and have a greater desire to consider change.

How to Make Behavior More Likely

In her TEDx talk, "How to Make a Behavior Addictive,"[17] Chance (based on the work on Tony Robbins) identifies six human needs that greatly influence the likelihood a behavior will consistently occur:

1. **Significance:** As humans, we need to feel who we are and what we do matters.
2. **Certainty:** At our core, we crave safety, security, and knowledge that our needs and expectations will be met.
3. **Uncertainty:** Paradoxically, we also desire novelty and variety. Intermittent reinforcement (the kind you get from a slot machine) maintains behavior better than consistent reinforcement (the kind you get from a vending machine—when it's working properly, anyway).
4. **Connection:** We need each other to survive and thrive.

5. **Growth:** We want to have a sense that we are moving forward.

6. **Contribution:** We long to feel like we are giving to others beyond ourselves.

Chance gives two examples of behavior that do and do not tap into these human needs: flash mobs and motorcycle helmets. Wearing a helmet while riding a motorcycle involves only the human need for certainty—a trait people aren't usually going for when they're riding a motorcycle! Because of this, it may be unlikely people will choose to wear a helmet on their own; thus, this behavior is regulated by law. On the other hand, flash mobs involve all six of these human needs, and despite being silly and kind of pointless, they have become incredibly popular.

What does all this have to do with imposterism? As we talked about at the beginning of the chapter, as individuals, we can cultivate community as a way to lift each other up and have the courage to do hard things even when we feel like imposters. We can also demonstrate a willingness to "be it even when we can't see it" so others will see it and be more likely to believe they can be it. What if we also got really brave and tried to actually *influence* organizational culture using some of the tools Zoe Chance teaches us? According to Chance, the greatest predictor of employee engagement and excitement is having a sense that they are making progress (which satisfies the human need for growth). Being an active part of an organization that prioritizes the recruitment, advancement, and retention of women, BIPOC, LGBTQIA+ folks, immigrants, and disabled individuals would certainly be an example of growth. It would also satisfy the human need for significance, uncertainty, connection, and contribution. Maybe we can start to have conversations with people in positions of power—to listen empathically and without a hidden agenda—and then use our human voices to suggest ideas or programs that cultivate the six human needs as a way to prioritize the inclusion and advancement of marginalized groups. If we *are* the people in power, we can spearhead the very same ideas. Any efforts we make to get people seats at the tables they have historically not been invited to should effectively reduce the experiences of imposterism and stereotype threat among those groups over time. They will be less likely to question whether they belong and in turn will no longer feel compelled to prove they do.

Importantly, the solutions we propose need to be desirable to the organization. According to organizational psychologist Adam Grant, people will ignore a problem if they are not fond of the solution.[18] Suggested programs that are perceived as restricting may be less welcomed than those that are seen as adding benefit or purpose. Owning the degree of problem complexity is also important to effecting change. Acknowledging that organizational and systemic bias are complex problems that are hard to solve won't scare your colleagues away; in fact, Grant suggests it will make them see you as more credible and may even trigger their curiosity so they will be more likely to get on board.

Having a community can lift you up and bolster your willingness to bravely go in a new direction even if few others have occupied a particular space before you. Together we can cultivate influence and full-size professional lives. Learning to embody self-compassion can also help pave the way.

The Recap: What to Know

- Humans crave connection, and the benefit of community is clear.
- There are many ways to cultivate community through current and new connections.
- Imposterism and stereotype threat interact in marginalized professionals.
- Even if you can't see it, you can definitely still be it.
- To be influential, listen, use your human voice (rather than your written word), and be transparent.
- Humans have six basic needs that make consistent behavior more likely: significance, certainty, uncertainty, connection, growth, and contribution.

The Work: What to Do

- Choose a strategy from the suggestions in this chapter to start cultivating a greater sense of community.
- Consider how you might influence your work culture to be more inclusive.

Chapter 13

Self-Compassion

You're already stuck with yourself for a lifetime. Why not improve this relationship?

—*Vironika Tugaleva*

Sara Schairer had been married for three years when her father was tragically killed by a truck while out jogging. Two years later, her daughter, Hannah, was born. Between deep grief and adjusting to new motherhood, life hadn't been easy, but Sara's marriage seemed to be weathering the storm. Or so she thought. Shortly before Hannah turned one, Sara's husband dropped a bomb: he wanted a divorce. His mind was made up, and he was unwilling to try couples counseling. Sara was devastated. For months, she worked on picking up the pieces of her life while navigating a divorce and caring for an infant mostly on her own. She felt in her bones she needed to turn her grief into something meaningful.

While Sara was home taking care of Hannah, she watched a lot of *The Ellen DeGeneres Show* while Hannah napped. Ellen, who ended every episode with her signature line, "Be kind to one another," interviewed author, therapist, and motivational speaker Wayne Dyer, who talked about the power of compassion to change the world.

210

This stuck with Sara. That evening she had a vision. She saw the word *compassionate* in a new form: *compassion it*. It was pronounced the same way, but her two-word version transformed the noun into a verb. For the next three years, Sara put her phrase into action. She practiced daily acts of compassion toward herself and others. "Verbifying" compassion led her to experience a powerful transformation in her suffering.

Sara initially created bumper stickers and wristbands to start spreading the word about *compassion it*, but she wanted to do something more impactful. She applied and was accepted to a year-long training program at Stanford's Center for Compassion and Altruism Research and Education (CCARE), where she became a certified compassion cultivation trainer. At first Sara struggled with imposterism. Nearly everyone in her CCARE training cohort was a licensed mental health professional, while her background was in marketing and sales. She frequently had thoughts like *Who am I to think it's my place to do this?* But by bringing self-compassion to her self-doubt and imposter feelings, Sara was able to forge ahead. She told me her imposterism provided "a healthy dose of humility and beginner's mind," which motivated her to keep learning. Once she began teaching compassion to others, she knew spreading the *compassion it* message was her calling. She went on to form a global nonprofit organization and social movement (www.compassionit.com) whose mission is to inspire compassionate action and attitudes around the world through education and advocacy. She also recently published her first book, *A Case for Compassion: What Happens When We Prioritize People and the Planet*.

What started as grief, devastation, depression, and lack of direction turned into a full-size passion-driven career. Not only does Sara spread compassion across the globe, but her personal practices have helped her thrive both personally and professionally. They can help you too.

SELF-CRITICISM

Your imposter voice is probably just one of many that stem from your inner critic, all of them colorful and specific versions of "I'm not good enough." As we talked about in chapter 7, this inner critic is designed to help or protect you in some way—maybe to keep you on your toes so you don't get complacent or to protect you from failure or humiliation. But it does a pretty lousy job. When brains perceive threat, they react to keep you safe. By now you're familiar with the fight/flight/freeze response that occurs when we perceive physical danger or even social threat. Snakes and coyotes regularly appeared where I used to live, and you can bet that when I came upon them, I hightailed it in the opposite direction. Danger averted. When you feel verbally attacked by a partner or friend, you might get defensive and fight back. Your mind does the very same thing in the form of your inner critic.[1] Only the perpetrator you're fighting is yourself.

If you perform poorly on an exam, at an interview, or delivering a presentation, your brain will perceive this as a threat: *Oh no, I failed, what if I never get into grad school or I get fired?* When your fight-or-flight system kicks in, where are you to go? Who are you to fight? As it turns out, we often turn this reaction inward on ourselves: *How could I be so stupid? I was so lazy not to prepare more. I deserve to fail.* This makes sense from a neurobiological standpoint, but fighting ourselves does not have the same helpful outcomes as fleeing from snakes and coyotes. In fact, research has shown that self-criticism is a maladaptive defense mechanism[2] that leads to underachievement and magnifies feelings of worthlessness, inferiority, and failure.[3] For example, in two prospective studies investigating the impact of self-criticism on academic, social, and health-related goals, higher levels of self-criticism were associated with lower goal achievement.[4]

In chapter 8 we talked about ways you can actively change your relationship with your inner critic so it no longer holds you back from pursuing a full-size life and career. The process of stepping back and observing your thoughts with detached curiosity creates a new context where choosing values becomes more accessible. You can also respond to your inner critic with *self-compassion* to achieve the same result.

SELF-COMPASSION

If a friend or colleague came to you, fretting about a recent work performance, would you respond with *How could you be so stupid? You deserve to fail!* If you did, I'm pretty sure you wouldn't have friends for very long. Intuitively, you know it is not OK or helpful to respond to those you care about in this manner when they are suffering. My podcast cohosts and I frequently text each other things like "I felt so much vitality during the interview, but I think I sounded like an inarticulate amateur." We respond to one another with texts like "It's hard to feel like that, but we are our own worst critics! I'm sure you sounded less like an amateur than your mind is telling you. I bet you'll sound very relatable to me." In other words, we are *validating and kind*. What might it be like to treat yourself the same way?

According to Paul Gilbert, psychologist and creator of compassion-focused therapy, compassion is about being aware of the suffering of self and others, with a commitment to do something to alleviate it. Compassion can flow in three directions: from you out to others, from others into you, and from you to yourself.[5] Compassion from you to yourself is *self-compassion*, a multidimensional construct consisting of three parts:[6]

1. Mindfulness of suffering
2. Common humanity
3. Self-kindness

We can learn to become aware of our present-moment suffering (mindfulness), connect with knowing we are not alone in our suffering (common humanity), and treat ourselves with kindness (self-kindness) instead of or in response to self-criticism. This can be particularly helpful during times of adversity, like when we feel like raging imposters.

The Face You Are Holding

Imagine the power of learning to treat yourself with compassion—of offering yourself kindness the way you so easily offer it to those you care about. I'd like you to bring to mind a human you love deeply. Imagine looking into this person's sweet face, and connect with how much you completely adore them. Maybe it's a child, partner, or grandparent. Imagine they say something like "I just feel so deeply flawed. Like I'm not enough. Like if people saw me for who I really am, they would reject and abandon me. I just know that at any moment, I'm going to be outed for the loser I really am." Take a moment to become deeply aware of their suffering, knowing they are not alone, because you suffer too, maybe in a very similar way. Imagine taking their face in your hands and looking into their eyes. What might you say to them in this moment that would offer genuine kindness? You don't have to talk them out of their thoughts. Despite being well intentioned, this can actually be experienced as invalidating. Instead, try something like "I'm here. Feeling this way is painful. You are not alone. You are worthy. You are loved exactly as you are." Now close your eyes, take a deep breath, and imagine that face you are holding is your own. Look into your own eyes, see the hurt there, and tell yourself, "I'm here. Feeling this way is painful. You are not alone. You are worthy. You are loved exactly as you are."

Sometimes when people first start to practice being kind to themselves, it can feel a little awkward or corny. But research has shown that self-compassion is associated with greater optimism,[7] resilience,[8] personal initiative, positive affect,[9] feelings of social connectedness,[10] and a greater sense of overall well-being and life satisfaction.[11] Self-compassion even buffers against social comparison[12] and low self-esteem: self-esteem fluctuates constantly and relies on social comparison—to have it, we have to believe we are better than others.[13] Self-compassion is different. It's practically the opposite because it focuses on connection with others—recognizing we suffer together. In fact, the root of the word *compassion* is "to suffer with."

You might think of self-criticism versus self-compassion like a nightmare boss versus a kind boss.[14] Let's say you report to these two bosses, and they give you a task you struggle to complete competently. Each boss gives you feedback. Boss #1 says, "Why couldn't you do this? You should know how to do this at this stage of your career. You need to get your act together!" Boss #2 says, "I can see this was a struggle for you. Show me what you need help with. We can do this together the first time so you can learn better for the next time." It seems pretty obvious that if you got to choose one boss, you'd opt for Boss #2—a person who will be more likely to contribute to your long-term professional growth and development. But when you talk to yourself, who do you sound more like? Probably Boss #1. Boss #1 is a jerk who does not facilitate your growth, motivation, or performance. Cultivating self-compassion means cultivating the Boss #2 within.

Notice in this example, too, Boss #2 isn't letting you off the hook. Often self-compassion is misunderstood in this way. Sometimes when people first learn about self-compassion, they worry they will relax their standards too much because self-kindness equates to not holding themselves accountable. But this couldn't be farther from the truth. Notice that Boss #2 isn't saying, "Eh, whatever, don't worry about it. Doing a bad job doesn't matter." They are kindly suggesting a way forward that will allow for development and promote motivation and success.

The Compassionate Letter[15]

James Pennebaker has been researching the powerful therapeutic effects of writing about emotional experiences since the 1980s.[16] We're going to take a page from his journal and do a letter-writing exercise together to help you cultivate compassion for yourself. While it can be tempting to say "I'll just be nicer to myself" and skip the experiential work, I want to encourage you to pause here and engage. My clients and I have found this exercise to be deeply impactful. It takes only a few minutes and will stick with you and make practicing self-compassion much easier in the long run. You are at a POP—who is the Me you want to be in this moment? Now take a minute to grab a pen and paper, as it is far more powerful to handwrite your letter than to type it on a computer or as a note in your phone. Start with "Dear [YOUR NAME]," then respond to the following four prompts in four short paragraphs. Don't worry about spelling or grammar or neatness. You can even just jot down bullet points if you prefer. But do write your responses out.

1. Using the second-person perspective (i.e., "you"), write down all the self-critical things your mind says to you, including your imposter thoughts—this awareness of your suffering is the first step to practicing self-compassion. For example, my letter might say, "Dear Jill, You are average. You are mediocre. There is nothing special about you. Everyone else is better than you. Any success you have achieved has been due to luck or help or fooling people into thinking you are competent. Pretty soon they will see you are not that smart or qualified, and the jig will be up."

2. Jot down a few sentences about when your inner critic and imposter voice showed up and what may have triggered it. Be sure to include experiences of marginalization that may relate. This expanded awareness and understanding can help foster self-kindness. For example, mine might say something like "You thought you were legit back in high school, when you were in the top 5 percent of your class and the president of the student council. But then a teacher called you a scatterbrain, and you got rejected from your top two colleges and had to settle for a mediocre state college. You had to get a master's from another mediocre state school to have any chance of getting into a doctoral program. When you managed to get into a highly

competitive graduate school where your dad knew the
director, the imposterism really took hold. That's when
you most feared you'd be outed as a fraud."

3. If you were to ask your inner imposter/critic what it is trying to do for you—how it might be trying to help or protect you—what might it say? How might you know you
are not alone in this (step two: common humanity)? For
example, my paragraph might read, "Maybe this imposter
voice is trying to keep you on your toes—to prevent you
from being complacent, because it knows you're capable of
contributing important things. Maybe it wants to protect
you from failure and humiliation. You are not alone. Most,
if not all, humans have an inner critic. Seventy percent have
an imposter voice. Even Maya Angelou and Meryl Streep
felt like frauds! You're in this together."

4. Think of a person, real or imaginary, who embodies tre-
mendous compassion. This person knows all of you—your
strengths and flaws—and accepts you just as you are. They
see your heart. If they read the first paragraph of your letter, what might they say to you (step three: self-kindness)?
Mine might say, "You are not alone in your suffering—
feeling like we are enough is a common human struggle
[reemphasizing common humanity]. You are working really
hard to contribute to the world. What you share through
therapy, writing, podcasting, and speaking is aimed at helping people. You regularly step out of your comfort zone in
service of reaching others. You may not feel special or that
you're making as big a splash as others, but you're doing
your best to make a difference. Even if it's a small difference, it matters and it's enough. You're enough."

Now sign the letter, then read it through slowly. Keep it somewhere where you can look back at it. Use it as a model for how you can practice the three elements of self-compassion: (1) mindfulness of your suffering, (2) common humanity, and (3) self-kindness.

COMPASSION FLOWING IN

I recently asked a therapy client about her relationship: "What do you do when your wife offers to help? If she offers to bring you a cup of coffee or tells you to sit down so she can finish up the dishes?" My client immediately became tearful. "I tell her, 'That's OK—don't worry about it. I can take care of it myself, thanks anyway.'" I asked about the tears. "This question moved you to tears. What's going on for you?" Still tearful, she responded, "I think I know where you're going with this. I talk about feeling alone and unsupported, like I'm juggling everything with no help. But when people *do* offer help, I have a really, really hard time accepting it. I don't know why it's so hard for me." She was right. That is exactly where I was going. I asked my client to pay attention to offers of compassion—when someone recognizes she is struggling, joins her, and offers kindness—and her responses to it. The following session, she reported back three observations: (1) she often didn't even notice when others were offering her kindness, (2) when she did notice, she felt vulnerable and guilty, so she mostly shut it down to get relief from those feelings, and (3) when she needed help, she found it nearly impossible to ask for it—the thought of asking for help triggered the most intense levels of guilt, vulnerability, and fear of judgment.

Often, the flow of compassion from you to others is the easiest to access, especially when the compassion is flowing to others you care about. As we discussed in the first part of the chapter, the flow of compassion from you to yourself—self-compassion—can be more challenging. Likewise, allowing the flow of compassion from others to yourself can often be challenging too.

Compassion Blocks and the Five As

I interviewed Dr. Michaela Thomas, psychologist and author of *The Lasting Connection: Developing Love and Compassion for Yourself and Your Partner.* She referred to the internal experiences that get in the way of allowing compassion to flow in as "compassion blocks." A block to asking for help, for example, might be a fear of being let down or a fear of closeness—in response, a person may put their guard up to avoid the uncomfortable feelings and the feared outcome. She noted this can happen with compassion flowing from anyone—romantic partners, friends, or coworkers alike.

In her book, Thomas recommends "The Five *As*" for overcoming blocks and allowing compassion to flow in:[17]

1. **Awareness:** Practice noticing when you are being offered kindness. Also notice any resistance that arises.
2. **Acknowledgment:** Acknowledge acts of kindness. Once you become aware that kindness is being offered and you may not be allowing it in, you can pivot to saying something like "I saw that you did the dishes after I went to bed with a headache last night" or "I noticed you parked the car off to the side so I could get by with the trash cans more easily."
3. **Acceptance:** Make space for the discomfort that arises around allowing compassion to flow in. Use the willingness skills you learned in earlier chapters to expand and allow your feelings and the kindness from others.

4. **Appreciation:** Express gratitude for the help and kindness you've been offered. "I really appreciate that you make the coffee every morning" or "It meant so much to me when you listened to me vent and validated my feelings."

5. **Asking:** Asking for help can be scary if you've been raised to be a "strong" man or a "superwoman" who juggles everything independently and with ease. Practice asking for help in small ways, and practice the techniques you learned earlier to observe and detach from unhelpful narratives.

Change is hard, but big, powerful transformations can start with just one step. Whether it's letting compassion flow in, practicing self-compassion, being willing, observing and unhooking from thoughts, or making valued choices, we can't wait until it *feels easy* to jump on board. We talked about the gap trap in chapter 8, wherein you get trapped and are unable to move forward because of a perceived gap in knowledge, experience, or expertise. Don't get trapped in self-criticism or doing everything alone because of a perceived gap in your ability to accept compassion flowing in from yourself and others. If you start practicing now, compassion will eventually feel more natural. Research on neuroplasticity teaches us this is true.[18]

Think of it like developing a good habit. As you repeat actions, the effect of your habits gets reinforced, and your self-image begins to change and shape your identity.[19] Instead of getting hooked by an "I'm just not the type of person who does compassion" narrative, try regularly practicing compassion, and you will start to see yourself differently.

While the ACT processes we've discussed thus far contain elements of compassion within them—acceptance means accepting yourself and your experience as it is, mindfulness teaches us to let go of judgment, observing thoughts helps us unhook from self-criticism, and values guide us to put what personally matters first—the practice of self-compassion and allowing compassion to flow in may offer its own additional benefits.[20] In at least one study, self-compassion was a strong mediator of ACT treatment outcome.[21] In other words, the degree to which participants improved in ACT was strongly influenced by self-compassion. I encourage you to make compassion practices a part of your expanding psychological flexibility repertoire. In the next and final chapter, we will review the tools you've learned and talk about how to keep going.

The Recap: What to Know
- Compassion flows in three directions: from you to others, from others to you, and from you to yourself.
- Self-compassion is composed of three parts: mindfulness of suffering, common humanity, and self-kindness.
- Self-compassion is a more effective motivator of behavior than self-criticism is.
- You can overcome compassion blocks by practicing the Five As: awareness, acknowledgment, acceptance, appreciation, and asking.

The Work: What to Do
- Picture yourself extending kindness to someone you care about, then imagine that person is you.
- Write yourself a compassionate letter.

Chapter 14

Keep Going

There is no greater threat to the critics and cynics and fearmongers
Than those of us who are willing to fall
Because we have learned how to rise

—*Brené Brown*

Growing up on the south side of Chicago, Michelle Robinson rode multiple buses to and from her charter high school, totaling three hours of commute time each day. She was an achiever—excellent grades, National Honor Society, and treasurer of her senior class. She set her sights on Princeton for college. When she shared her aspirations with her school guidance counselor, the counselor smirked and said, "I'm not sure that you are Princeton material." This dismissive and patronizing statement had the potential to plant a seed of self-doubt in Michelle—it could have caused her to lower her expectations and goals. But rather than allow one person's unsubstantiated opinion to change her opinion of herself, she sought support from her neighbor and assistant principal, Mr. Jones, who had always trusted and believed in Michelle. He wrote her a letter of recommendation, which, along with her remaining application materials, did the trick: she was accepted to Princeton as an undergrad, and later to Harvard Law School.

Today, Michelle Robinson Obama has rubbed elbows with the world's most extraordinary people. Each of them has had doubters and critics who have loudly and publicly attempted to cut them down at every turn. What Michelle has learned is that the nay-sayers never go away, but the most successful people learn how to live with the noise and push forward with their goals, leaning on the supportive people they have met along the way. Michelle never returned to her high school to tell that counselor she was indeed Princeton material—she realized she had nothing to prove to that woman, only to herself.

Now here *you* are, thirteen chapters later, with a new set of knowledge and skills. You have learned various ways to build psychological flexibility. You understand now that your thoughts and feelings are not the enemy—that trying to avoid or control them is what keeps you stuck. You have learned to change your relationship with those internal experiences—accepting feelings and observing thoughts—so that you are free to choose values-congruent actions that add up to a full-size professional life. You have learned the benefits of self-compassion and the value of culti-vating community.

Your pain and challenges will never disappear. They are just part of the deal for us humans. You will encounter naysayers—like Michelle Obama's guidance counselor, or your own inner critic and imposter voice—but you now have the tools to manage whatever they trigger and to continue onward with the goals that most deeply matter to you.

A FINAL TOUR OF PSYCHOLOGICAL FLEXIBILITY

Let's walk through a final example of how I used my own psychological flexibility skills when a professional opportunity triggered big, uncomfortable feelings and massive amounts of self-doubt and imposterism. You can use this as a model for what practicing everything you have learned might look like in a specific situation. I will walk you through how I was feeling, what I was thinking, and what I did (or didn't do) in response.

When my friend and colleague Lynn tagged me in a comment on the Facebook page of Allison, a woman who raised capital for nonprofit organizations, I clicked the link. I had nothing to do with nonprofits or fundraising, so my curiosity was piqued. It was an application to do a TEDx talk, and the deadline was that day. This was a professional dream of mine—like top-of-the-bucket-list dream.

Can I do this? Do I have "an idea worth sharing"? Well, there's no harm in applying—they say everyone gets rejected the first few times they apply anyway. Might as well get my first rejection over with.

I applied that day, a Monday. Allison asked for a five-minute video audition, and she wanted it by Friday. After three days and at least eleven takes, sitting at my computer alone on Zoom with my ring light on, I sent her the file. That afternoon I received the email: "Welcome to TEDxLenoxVillageWomen!" The virtual event was being held four weeks later; the final video was due in two.

How the hell did I get this? She was obviously short on submissions and must have just accepted everyone. I've grown three more chins and gone up two sizes during this pandemic, and now I have to forever memorialize myself in a TEDx video? I don't think I can do this. Although, I'm sure no one is going to watch it anyway, so maybe the weight doesn't matter.

DAMN, Sheila. She was the mouthiest she'd been in a long while—of course she was. You don't get an unexpected opportunity to check a huge professional dream off your bucket list without your inner critic having something to say about it. I asked myself "WWOD"—what would Oprah do?—and "WWOS"—what would Oprah say?

Pipe down, Sheila. I've got this. I know you're just looking out for me. You don't want me to fall flat on my face, to fail, to humiliate myself. That matters to us. But so do courage, willingness, vulnerability, and living a full-size life. Oprah would do this talk and not let her insecurities stop her. If she knew I was struggling, she would tell me, "Jill, you are so much more than your body—you have a message to share, so share it."

I put my full talk together. I bought a bold red shirt and wore leopard-print shoes because I wasn't going to hide behind my insecurity about not wanting to be seen. I hired a video guy to help me create a professional-looking video since the pandemic-era event wouldn't be happening on a live TED stage. I even bought a small circular red rug to stand on so I could feel a smidge like I was having a true TED experience. Ezra (the video guy) and I met at a hip studio space in Long Beach. It had exposed brick walls and original hardwood floors. The space exuded confidence—if a space can do that—which I failed to absorb.

Despite speaking to an audience of exactly one, my hands shook and my breath was shallow. I took it one time through, using a teleprompter, then did a few more takes with a little direction from Ezra.

He hates it. He's barely saying anything. When I practiced on the phone with a friend, she barely said anything either. Billy was a little more positive, but I'm sure he was just being nice; husbands have to be nice. Oh my god, it's terrible.

Thank you, Sheila. I reminded her why we were doing this—about our values.

It is our mission to share psychological flexibility skills with others. To reach those who may not have the resources or desire to see a therapist. If it flops, gets no views, or gets views but is met with crickets or criticism, we still showed up with courage and willingness in service of that mission.

I validated my feelings, reminded myself about common humanity, and extended myself some kindness.

This is scary, but you're not alone. You can do this.

Ezra edited the video and sent it to me within days. I was both nervous and excited to watch it. I still felt so much uncertainty about the talk, and no one ever likes to see themselves on video.

OMG, you look huge, Little Tubbette! Why didn't you tuck your shirt in? Your talk was only eleven and a half minutes—real TED speakers use their full eighteen minutes. *This idea is so cliché. If anyone even watches, they'll all be thinking,* Been there, done that, nothing new being added here. *It's not too late to back out. You don't have to humiliate yourself like this.*

I sang the first line of the chorus to the Ready for the World song: "Oh. Oh, Sheila. Let me love you till the morning comes." I reminded her that if we are this panicked, we are right where we are supposed to be. That the bright red neon arrow is here, and it is pointing → *this way* to what matters! I told her again, *We've got this. If this message speaks to even one person whose life—or even just whose day—is strengthened by it, we have lived our values. Even if it's a spectacular flop, we showed up, we were brave, WE DID A TED TALK! We've got this.*

After a couple of minor back-and-forths with Ezra, I sent

Allison the video. Still, Sheila didn't quit. Not then, not when the event occurred in front of a modest audience of about a hundred (the platform maxed out and wouldn't let anyone else attend, which was both a disappointment and a relief), not when the TEDx YouTube channel released the talk.

I felt so scared putting myself out there. I made space for it. I felt incredibly vulnerable. I used my breath to slow down, to open and allow the experience in its entirety. I reminded myself to hold the outcome lightly—that the choice to show up and take action in line with my values was the only part I got to control. Then I started sharing the talk. I shared it on Twitter, Instagram, Facebook, and LinkedIn. I felt sick with dread, sensing how painful silence would be. I knew it was unlikely a bunch of people would actually *say*, "That was shit," but it felt like silence would confirm it. When people like things, they say so.

Sheila started up again, this time with *You're a braggart. Who do you think you are, promoting yourself in this way? You're embarrassing yourself.*

At the writing of this chapter, the talk has had just over four thousand views on YouTube. It didn't go viral and make me an overnight sensation. Nor did it completely flop. I got feedback from a handful of people who shared how meaningful the message was for them, that it was memorable, and that they intended to share it with others. I even got one "mic drop" comment and mind-blown emoji. Those meant a lot. They are who I did it for. For them and for me.

I did it. It was painful. And so, so worth it. When I rewatch my talk, Sheila watches it with me, pointing out the things I should have done differently—the places I looked stiff or sounded inauthentic. Sheila criticizes my appearance. But I—the "I" that is unhooked and distinct from Sheila—can watch the woman on that screen, in her bold red blouse and leopard-print heels, and see her courage, her willingness, her giant leap toward the Me she wants to be. As she wraps up her talk, pointing out that *me* sits inside *moment*, I think, *She was the Me she wanted to be in that moment. She practiced what she preaches. And that is something to be pretty damn proud of.*

The Bad News

I have been living ACT and building psychological flexibility for more than twenty years, and my critical imposter voice is still here. Remember, psychological flexibility is not about controlling your thoughts and feelings. It's about living a full-size life in service of your values—the Me you most deeply desire to be— bringing those thoughts and feelings along for the ride. When you lean in to the things you want, the things that matter to you, the things that you long for, you invite vulnerability. The more it matters, the more you have to lose and the more anxious and full of self-doubt and imposterism you might feel. As you move up in your career, you don't prove your imposter wrong. On the contrary, you are expected to be more of an expert even if you don't *feel* like you actually are.

The Good News

Alongside my imposterism and feelings of anxiety, I also feel more alive than I've ever felt. There is power, pride, mastery, accomplishment, surprise, and wonder in going after what you want, in living full-size over fun-size.

You are now equipped to walk this path too. You have the wisdom to identify the Me you want to be in each moment. You understand what typically gets in the way—responding to self-limiting beliefs and painful emotions on autopilot—and that avoiding emotional pain makes you feel better in the short term but keeps you stuck in the long term. You have the skills to practice willingness toward that pain instead—to open and allow the discomfort in service of leaning into all that you long for. You can now be a curious and dispassionate observer of your thoughts and self-stories rather than be bossed around by them in unhelpful ways. You can respond to your inner critic by letting compassion flow in from others and from yourself, and you can connect with your community for added support.

Hopefully you have already stretched outside your comfort zone, using the skills you've acquired to overcome the obstacles that used to get in your way. But you've probably failed to do so on several occasions too. So have I, probably even today (if not yet, I'm sure to later). But as boxer Sugar Ray Leonard is thought to have said, "If you never know failure, you will never know success." Failure helps us learn, and developing psychological flexibility is an ongoing process. There are no arrivals at "Aha! I've done it! I'm now psychologically flexible!" Responding to vulnerability and other challenging internal experiences is something we have to return to again and again, each time a choice is made (so basically all day, every day!)

Change in some domains will come more easily than in others. I'm able to practice being psychologically flexible fairly well in my professional and writing life, but I still struggle to practice it as a parent. However, when I lose my patience with my kids in one moment, I get to choose the Me I want to be in the very next, and can apologize, setting an example of someone who takes responsibility for her mistakes (a value). My badass healthcare-CEO friend Marie who you read about in chapter 12 struggles most at work. After more than twenty-five years in the industry and despite an impressive résumé with titles like vice president, founder, and CEO, she still worries about her lack of graduate education. She even asked me, "How do you know if you have imposter 'syndrome,' or if you're really an imposter?" She asked because she thought she was! And yet she has leaned on her community by joining organizations like Chief, a private network of female leaders, and Portfolia, a group of all-women investors, to give her the courage to forge ahead even when she feels out of her depth.

Have patience with yourself. Think of yourself like an oak tree. An oak is a slower-growing tree, and slower-growing trees are stronger trees. Or like a river birch. A river birch has a flexible limb structure, which means it bends but does not break. What's more, when high winds cause a river birch to bend, this builds additional structures on the inside of the tree, thereby fortifying it and making it stronger. So grow slowly and practice flexibility when the winds pick up. You will be on your way to growing stronger and living full-size before you know it.

HOW THIS WORK IS DIFFERENT

Many books about success and growth focus on setting goals—often SMART goals, meaning they are specific, measurable, attainable, relevant, and time based—and that can certainly be helpful. But while we can set SMART professional goals—like to write a monthly newsletter or prepare a TEDx talk—we truly have no control over what happens beyond the process of writing and preparing. We can have all the talent in the world, learn about our industries, write the world's best content, and still not hit the subscriber number we hope to or have our TEDx talk accepted. As professionals, we need to be deeply connected to our why. The why is how we keep showing up. The why—along with our new relationship with thoughts and feelings—is how we persevere through disappointment, self-doubt, frustration, and envy. And persevering—showing up—is the only way to make our desired outcome more likely, even if it will never be a guarantee.

As we draw close to the end, let's pause for a reminder of why. Consider a goal, and then ask yourself *why* you want to achieve it. Write down your answer, either in long form or in simple bullet points. When you encounter one more rejection or watch someone else achieve a professional milestone you've been dreaming about (maybe even someone you know to be less talented or hardworking than you), when no one comments on your post, or when your mind tells you you're not enough or you're a fraud and tries to talk you out of pursuing your dreams, what's going to keep you persevering and moving forward? Why will you keep moving forward?

When Michelangelo was asked how he created great sculptures like *David*, he explained that he imagined the finished sculpture already existed inside the block of marble. Then he chipped away little by little to reveal what was already there. The people you imagine are somehow smarter, better, or more successful than you don't have a slew of qualities you don't. They've just chipped away at what is obscuring the best versions of themselves. You can use your newly acquired psychological flexibility skills to chip away at your experiential avoidance to reveal a bold, brave, willing-to-be-vulnerable version of yourself—the full-size you.

ALLOW ME TO PAVE THE WAY

When child psychologist and assistant professor Kim Gushanas was invited to teach ACT to medical students, she felt anxious and under pressure. It was her first year as a faculty member in the department of psychiatry, and she was intimidated by the MDs. *Who am I to be teaching medical students?* she thought. *They don't care about psychology.* She was teaching physicians who wanted to be more humanistic in their practice, yet her brain told her they would not value what she had to offer. Despite a strong background in medical psychology research and practice, she considered reaching out to the director to suggest they bring in someone with more expertise.

Then she caught herself.

Kim got present and became aware of the uncomfortable feelings she was trying to avoid and the self-critical thoughts that were hooking her. She made space for the anxiety and self-doubt, recognizing that she didn't have to *feel* confident to be able to move forward if doing so mattered to her. She observed her imposter thoughts in a curious and detached way, realizing they were trying to protect her from failure but were not helping her live full-size. She connected to her values. Specifically, Kim's professional mission is to usher modern science and evidence-based practice into historically traditional educational spaces (like her psychoanalytically leaning psychiatry program). She told herself, *Even if I plant just a small seed that they find useful, this will be worth doing.* She realized she had to do it for herself, in service of her values, despite the fear and imposterism. Kim harnessed psychological flexibility to be the Me she most deeply desired to be.

One hundred medical students and a dozen faculty members

attended Kim's talk. During our interview, her anxiety returned simply as a result of recounting the experience. When I asked how the talk went, Kim said she thought it went well, but the fact was she didn't get any feedback. She had to sit with the uncertainty of not *really* knowing how it was received. Nonetheless, she felt great that she chose to follow through with it. Yes, she was anxious, intimidated, and full of self-doubt and imposter feelings. *And* she felt proud, empowered, and accomplished. We can think and feel many ways all at once and choose to act based on values no matter what.

How can you do the same? Your psychological flexibility skills can be summed up in one easy-to-remember acronym, PAVE:

P: Pause and get present—take a deep, mindful breath and become aware of your thoughts and feelings.

A: Accept—make space for uncomfortable internal experiences, letting go of judgment and resistance.

V: Values—identify what matters and the Me you most deeply wish to be in this moment.

E: Execute—move your hands, feet, or mouth (the only things you get to control) in the direction of your values.

I like to think of psychologically flexible living as showing up to each moment as your personally chosen, fully authentic self. How do you know if you're showing up authentically? Think of it like really good branding. When someone has a solid brand strategy, their design is immediately recognizable—you know who you are dealing with without needing them to identify themselves. When I come across a Brené Brown social media post, I know it's her because the fonts, colors, shapes, textures, lines, and positive and negative space tell me so. Think of these design elements like the values that make up your authentic self. What does your metaphorical brand deck look like? Title font = openness; main body font = honesty; script font = playfulness; hex colors = curious, adventurous, brave, bold; company logo = integrity. You can consistently employ your branding design to show up as your easy-to-recognize, authentic, psychologically flexible self.

In *Life Lessons*, Elisabeth Kübler-Ross and David Kessler identify the fourteen most important lessons they learned from decades of talking with people who were dying.[1] These lessons aim to solve what Kübler-Ross called the single biggest problem in life: unfinished business. The lessons—things like love, authenticity, and play—are meant to encourage the living to finish their business now. In much the same way, you can choose to stop living fun-size—to change your relationship with your inner world so it no longer holds you back—and you can pursue a life that deeply matters to you before it's too late.

Now get out there and keep going.

Notes

Chapter 1: You Might Be a Fraud

1. Pauline Rose Clance and Suzanne Ament Imes, "The Impostor Phenomenon in High Achieving Women," *Psychotherapy Theory, Research and Practice* 15, no. 3 (1978): 1–8; J. Kruger and D. Dunning, "Unskilled and Unaware of It: How Difficulties in Recognizing One's Own Incompetence Lead to Inflated Self-Assessments," *Journal of Personality and Social Psychology* 77, no. 6 (1999): 1121–1134.
2. R. O. McElwee and Tricia J. Yurak, "The Phenomenology of the Impostor Phenomenon," *Individual Differences Research* 8, no. 3 (2010): 184–197.
3. Clance and Imes, "The Impostor Phenomenon," 1–8; Kruger and Dunning, "Unskilled and Unaware of It," 1121–1134.
4. Valerie Young, *The Secret Thoughts of Successful Women: Why Capable People Suffer from the Impostor Syndrome and How to Thrive in Spite of It* (Crown Business, 2011); Adam Grant, *Think Again: The Power of Knowing What You Don't Know* (Viking, 2021).
5. Kruger and Dunning, "Unskilled and Unaware of It," 1121–1134.
6. Janet Helms, *The Power Dynamics of White Racial Identity in Social Interactions* (plenary address, Association for Contextual Behavioral Science World Conference, Dublin, June 28, 2019).
7. Kevin Cokley, Shannon McClain, Alicia Enciso, and Mercedes Martinez, "An Examination of the Impact of Minority Status Stress and Impostor Feelings on the Mental Health of Diverse Ethnic Minority College Students," *Journal of Multicultural Counseling and Development* 41, no. 2 (2013): 82–95.
8. Clance and Imes, "The Impostor Phenomenon," 1–8; Kruger and Dunning, "Unskilled and Unaware of It," 1121–1134; Valerie Young, *The Secret Thoughts of Successful Women*; Sijia Li, Jennifer L. Hughes, and Su Myat Thu, "The Links Between Parenting Styles and Imposter Phenomenon," *Psi Chi Journal of Psychological Research* 19, no. 2 (2014).
9. Dena M. Bravata, Sharon A. Watts, Autumn L. Keefer, Divya K. Madhusudhan, Katie T. Taylor, Dani M. Clark, Ross S. Nelson, Kevin O. Cokley,

and Heather K. Hagg, "Prevalence, Predictors, and Treatment of Impostor Syndrome: A Systematic Review," *Journal of General Internal Medicine* 35, no. 4 (2020): 1252–1275.

10. Rebecca L. Badawy, Brooke A. Gazdag, Jeffrey R. Bentley, and Robyn L. Brouer, "Are All Impostors Created Equal? Exploring Gender Differences in the Impostor Phenomenon-Performance Link," *Personality and Individual Differences* 131 (2018): 156–163.

11. Ruchika Tulshyan and Jodi-Ann Burey, "Stop Telling Women They Have Imposter Syndrome," *Harvard Business Review* (February 11, 2021), https://hbr. org/2021/02/stop-telling-women-they-have-imposter-syndrome.

12. Jeffrey E. Young, Janet S. Klosko, and Marjorie E. Weishaar, *Schema Therapy* (New York: Guilford, 2003), 254.

13. Yuval Noah Harari, *Sapiens: A Brief History of Humankind* (New York: Harper, 2014).

Chapter 2: What Type of Imposter Are You?

1. Jill A. Stoddard and Niloofar Afari, *The Big Book of ACT Metaphors: A Practitioner's Guide to Experiential Exercises and Metaphors in Acceptance and Commitment Therapy* (New Harbinger Publications, 2014).

2. Valerie Young, *The Secret Thoughts of Successful Women: Why Capable People Suffer from the Impostor Syndrome and How to Thrive in Spite of It* (Crown Business, 2011).

3. Michael Herold, "What If I Had a Time Machine?," TEDxVienna video, filmed in 2015, https://www.youtube.com/watch?v=dbx_rzZYH5Q.

4. Carol S. Dweck, *Mindset: The New Psychology of Success* (Random House Digital, 2008).

5. Janina Scarlet, "Superwomen: Discovering Our Inner Superpowers," TEDxLenoxVillageWomen video, filmed in 2020, https://www.ted.com/talks/janina_scarlet_ph_d_super_women_discovering_our_inner_superpowers; Janina Scarlet, "This Is Your Origin Story," TEDxAkitaIntlU video, filmed in 2020, https://www.ted.com/talks/janina_scarlet_this_is_your_origin_story.

6. Young, *The Secret Thoughts of Successful Women*, 130.

Chapter 3: There Is No Cure (but There Is an Alternative)

1. Valerie Young, *The Secret Thoughts of Successful Women: Why Capable People Suffer from the Impostor Syndrome and How to Thrive in Spite of It* (Crown Business, 2011).

2. Young, *The Secret Thoughts of Successful Women*, 19.

3. Ruchika Tulshyan and Jodi-Ann Burey, "Stop Telling Women They Have Imposter Syndrome," *Harvard Business Review* (February 11, 2021), https://hbr. org/2021/02/stop-telling-women-they-have-imposter-syndrome.

4. Alicia Menendez, *The Likability Trap* (Harper Business, 2019).

5. Young, *The Secret Thoughts of Successful Women*.

6. Tomas Chamorro-Premuzic, *Why Do So Many Incompetent Men Become Leaders? (And How to Fix It)* (Harvard Business Press, 2019).

7. Basima A. Tewfik, "The Impostor Phenomenon Revisited: Examining the Relationship Between Workplace Impostor Thoughts and Interpersonal Effectiveness at Work," *Academy of Management Journal* 65, no. 3 (June 2022).

8. Basima Tewfik, "Found Out or Psyched Up: How and When Workplace Impostor Thoughts Breed Mastery at Work," *Academy of Management Proceedings* 2020, no. 1 (August 2020): 11648.

9. Adam Grant, *Think Again: The Power of Knowing What You Don't Know* (Viking, 2021).

10. Tara Mohr, *Playing Big: Find Your Voice, Your Mission, Your Message* (Avery, 2015).

11. Steven C. Hayes, Kirk D. Strosahl, and Kelly G. Wilson, *Acceptance and Commitment Therapy: The Process and Practice of Mindful Change* (Guilford, 2011).

12. Andrew T. Gloster, Noemi Walder, Michael Levin, Michael Twohig, and Maria Karekla, "The Empirical Status of Acceptance and Commitment Therapy: A Review of Meta-Analyses," *Journal of Contextual Behavioral Science* 18 (October 2020): 181–192.

13. Hayes, Strosahl, and Wilson, *Acceptance and Commitment Therapy.*

14. Amrisha Vaish, Tobias Grossmann, and Amanda Woodward, "Not All Emotions Are Created Equal: The Negativity Bias in Social-Emotional Development," *Psychological Bulletin* 134, no. 3 (2008): 383.

15. Katherine Vytal and Stephan Hamann, "Neuroimaging Support for Discrete Neural Correlates of Basic Emotions: A Voxel-Based Meta-Analysis," *Journal of Cognitive Neuroscience* 22, no. 12 (2010): 2864–2885.

16. Päivi Lappalainen, Katariina Keinonen, Inka Pakkala, Raimo Lappalainen, and Riku Nikander, "The Role of Thought Suppression and Psychological Inflexibility in Older Family Caregivers' Psychological Symptoms and Quality of Life," *Journal of Contextual Behavioral Science* 20 (2021): 129–136.

Chapter 4: Getting off Autopilot: The Gift of Presence

1. Joel Hoomans, "35,000 Decisions: The Great Choices of Strategic Leaders," *Leading Edge*, March 20, 2015, https://go.roberts.edu/leadingedge/the-great-choices-of-strategic-leaders.

2. Daniel Kahneman, *Thinking, Fast and Slow* (Macmillan, 2011).

3. Kendra Cherry, "How We Use Selective Attention to Filter Information and Focus," *Verywell Mind*, June 10, 2022, https://www.verywellmind.com/what-is-selective-attention-2795022#:~:text=Selective%20attention%20is%20the%20process,and%20focus%20on%20what%20matters.

4. Daniel J. Schad and Ralf Engbert, "The Zoom Lens of Attention: Simulating Shuffled Versus Normal Text Reading Using the SWIFT Model," *Visual Cognition* 20, no. 4–5 (2012): 391–421.

5. Jordana Cepelewicz, "To Pay Attention, the Brain Uses Filters, Not a Spotlight," *Quanta Magazine*, September 24, 2019, https://www.quantamagazine.org/to-pay-attention-the-brain-uses-filters-not-a-spotlight-20190924/

6. Yair Bar-Haim, Dominique Lamy, Lee Pergamin, Marian J. Bakermans-Kranenburg, and Marinus H. Van Ijzendoorn, "Threat-Related Attentional Bias in Anxious and Nonanxious Individuals: A Meta-Analytic Study," *Psychological Bulletin* 133, no. 1 (2007): 1.

7. Brené Brown, *The Call to Courage*, 2019, Netflix special, https://www.netflix.com/title/81010166.

8. Jon Kabat Zinn, "Wherever You Go, There You Are: Mindfulness Meditation in Everyday Life," *Hyperion* (1994): 78–80.

9. Ruth Q. Wolever, Kyra J. Bobinet, Kelley McCabe, Elizabeth R. Mackenzie, Erin Fekete, Catherine A. Kusnick, and Michael Baime, "Effective and Viable Mind-Body Stress Reduction in the Workplace: A Randomized Controlled Trial," *Journal of Occupational Health Psychology* 17, no. 2 (2012): 246.

10. Rollin McCraty, Mike Atkinson, and Dana Tomasino, "Impact of a Workplace Stress Reduction Program on Blood Pressure and Emotional Health in Hypertensive Employees," *Journal of Alternative and Complementary Medicine* 9, no. 3 (June 2003): 355–369.

11. Anna F. Dawson, William W. Brown, Joanna Anderson, Bella Datta, James N. Donald, Karen Hong, Sophie Allan, Tom B. Mole, Peter B. Jones, and Julieta Galante, "Mindfulness-Based Interventions for University Students: A Systematic Review and Meta-Analysis of Randomised Controlled Trials," *Applied Psychology: Health and Well-Being* 12, no. 2 (2020): 384–410; Dawn Querstret, Linda Morison, Sophie Dickinson, Mark Cropley, and Mary John, "Mindfulness-Based Stress Reduction and Mindfulness-Based Cognitive Therapy for Psychological Health and Well-Being in Nonclinical Samples: A Systematic Review and Meta-Analysis," *International Journal of Stress Management* 27, no. 4 (2020): 394–411.

12. Jon Kabat-Zinn, "An Outpatient Program in Behavioral Medicine for Chronic Pain Patients Based on the Practice of Mindfulness Meditation: Theoretical Considerations and Preliminary Results," *General Hospital Psychiatry* 4, no. 1 (1982): 33–47.

13. Jon Kabat-Zinn, Elizabeth Wheeler, Timothy Light, Anne Skillings, Mark J. Scharf, Thomas G. Cropley, David Hosmer, and Jeffrey D. Bernhard, "Influence of a Mindfulness Meditation-Based Stress Reduction Intervention on Rates of Skin Clearing in Patients with Moderate to Severe Psoriasis Undergoing Photo Therapy (UVB) and Photochemotherapy (PUVA)," *Psychosomatic Medicine* 60, no. 5 (1998): 625–632.

14. Kenneth H. Kaplan, Don L. Goldenberg, and Maureen Galvin-Nadeau, "The Impact of a Meditation-Based Stress Reduction Program on Fibromyalgia," *General Hospital Psychiatry* 15, no. 5 (1993): 284–289.

15. Molly Cairncross and Carlin J. Miller, "The Effectiveness of Mindfulness-Based Therapies for ADHD: A Meta-Analytic Review," *Journal of Attention Disorders* 24, no. 5 (2020): 627–643.

16. Nora Suleiman-Martos, Jose L. Gomez-Urquiza, Raimundo Aguayo-Estremera, Guillermo A. Cañadas-De La Fuente, Emilia I. De La Fuente-Solana, and Luis Albendín-García, "The Effect of Mindfulness Training on Burnout Syndrome in Nursing: A Systematic Review and Meta-Analysis," *Journal of Advanced Nursing* 76, no. 5 (2020): 1124–1140.

17. Patrick K. Hyland, R. Andrew Lee, and Maura J. Mills, "Mindfulness at Work: A New Approach to Improving Individual and Organizational Performance," *Industrial and Organizational Psychology* 8, no. 4 (2015): 576–602.

18. Theresa M. Glomb, Michelle K. Duffy, Joyce E. Bono, and Tao Yang, "Mindfulness at Work," in *Research in Personnel and Human Resources Management*, ed. Aparna Joshi, Hui Liao, and Joseph J. Martocchio (Emerald Publishing, 2011), 30:115–157.

19. David M. Levy, Jacob O. Wobbrock, Alfred W. Kasczniak, and Marilyn Ostergren, "The Effects of Mindfulness Meditation Training on Multitasking in a High-Stress Information Environment," in *Proceedings of Graphics Interface 2012* (Canadian Information Processing Society, 2012), 45–52.

20. Chad Dube, Caren M. Rotello, and Evan Heit, "Assessing the Belief Bias Effect with ROCs: It's a Response Bias Effect," *Psychological Review* 117, no. 3 (2010): 831.

21. Richard J. Davidson, Jon Kabat-Zinn, Jessica Schumacher, Melissa Rosenkranz, Daniel Muller, Saki F. Santorelli, Ferris Urbanowski, Anne Harrington, Katherine Bonus, and John F. Sheridan, "Alterations in Brain and Immune Function Produced by Mindfulness Meditation," *Psychosomatic Medicine* 65, no. 4 (2003): 564–570.

22. Meredith Wilson, "Chicken Fat," Capitol Records, 1962.

23. Tara Brach, "Tara Talks: Pain x Resistance = Suffering," released on May 2, 2018, YouTube video, https://youtu.be/3JywTh5O8ys.

24. Elisabeth Kübler-Ross and David Kessler, *Life Lessons: Two Experts on Death and Dying Teach Us About the Mysteries of Life and Living* (Simon and Schuster, 2012).

Chapter 5: Keep Your Why Close By: Getting Clear on What It's All For

1. Kathryn E. Williams, Joseph Ciarrochi, and Patrick CL Heaven, "Inflexible Parents, Inflexible Kids: A 6-Year Longitudinal Study of Parenting Style and the Development of Psychological Flexibility in Adolescents," *Journal of Youth and Adolescence* 41, no. 8 (2012): 1053–1066.

2. Jenna LeJeune and Jason B. Luoma, *Values in Therapy: A Clinician's Guide to Helping Clients Explore Values, Increase Psychological Flexibility, and Live a More Meaningful Life* (New Harbinger Publications, 2019).

3. Andrew T. Gloster, Jens Klotsche, Joseph Ciarrochi, Georg Eifert, Rainer Sonntag, Hans-Ulrich Wittchen, and Jürgen Hoyer, "Increasing Valued Behaviors Precedes Reduction in Suffering: Findings from a Randomized Controlled Trial Using ACT," *Behaviour Research and Therapy* 91 (2017): 64–71.
4. Jack Brehm, *A Theory of Psychological Reactance* (Academic Press, 1966).
5. LeJeune and Luoma, *Values in Therapy.*
6. John T. Blackledge and Steven C. Hayes, "Emotion Regulation in Acceptance and Commitment Therapy," *Journal of Clinical Psychology* 57, no. 2 (2001): 243–255.
7. Steven C. Hayes, Kirk D. Strosahl, and Kelly G. Wilson, *Acceptance and Commitment Therapy: The Process and Practice of Mindful Change* (Guilford, 2011).
8. LeJeune and Luoma, *Values in Therapy.*
9. Yael Schonbrun, Debbie Sorensen, and Jill Stoddard, "Values During Times of Transition," February 16, 2022, in *Psychologists off the Clock*, podcast, https://offtheclockpsych.com/238-values-transition/.
10. Steven C. Hayes, *Get Out of Your Mind and Into Your Life: The New Acceptance and Commitment Therapy* (New Harbinger Publications, 2005).

Chapter 6: Holding Outcomes Lightly

1. James Clear, *Atomic Habits: An Easy & Proven Way to Build Good Habits & Break Bad Ones* (Penguin, 2018), 33.
2. Ayelet Fishbach, *Get It Done: Surprising Lessons from the Science of Motivation* (Little, Brown Spark, 2022).
3. Jill A. Stoddard and Niloofar Afari, *The Big Book of ACT Metaphors: A Practitioner's Guide to Experiential Exercises and Metaphors in Acceptance and Commitment Therapy* (New Harbinger Publications, 2014).
4. Jenna LeJeune and Jason B. Luoma, *Values in Therapy: A Clinician's Guide to Helping Clients Explore Values, Increase Psychological Flexibility, and Live a More Meaningful Life* (New Harbinger Publications, 2019).
5. Fishbach, *Get It Done.*

Chapter 7: The Harsh Inner Critic

1. John T. Cacioppo, Stephanie Cacioppo, and Jackie K. Gollan, "The Negativity Bias: Conceptualization, Quantification, and Individual Differences," *Behavioral and Brain Sciences* 37, no. 3 (2014): 309.
2. Richard M. Wenzlaff and Daniel M. Wegner, "Thought Suppression," *Annual Review of Psychology* 51, no. 1 (2000): 59–91.
3. Daniel M. Wegner, David J. Schneider, Samuel R. Carter, and Teri L. White, "Paradoxical Effects of Thought Suppression," *Journal of Personality and Social Psychology* 53, no. 1 (1987): 5.
4. Julie Tseng and Jordan Poppenk, "Brain Meta-State Transitions Demarcate

Thoughts Across Task Contexts Exposing the Mental Noise of Trait Neuroticism," *Nature Communications* 11, no. 1 (2020): 1–12.

5. Amrisha Vaish, Tobias Grossmann, and Amanda Woodward, "Not All Emotions Are Created Equal: The Negativity Bias in Social-Emotional Development," *Psychological Bulletin* 134, no. 3 (2008): 383.

6. Jeffrey E. Young, Janet S. Klosko, and Marjorie E. Weishaar, *Schema Therapy* (New York: Guilford, 2003), 254.

7. Julie Lythcott-Haims, "A Doctor Held Me Hostage for Thirty Years: I'm Ridding Myself of His Grasp," *Julie's Pod*, November 28, 2021, https://jlythcotthaims.bulletin.com/328375265376011.

8. Cacioppo, Cacioppo, and Gollan, "The Negativity Bias," 309.

Chapter 8: Choosing When to Listen (and How Not To)

1. Michael W. Eysenck, Karin Mogg, Jon May, Anne Richards, and Andrew Mathews, "Bias in Interpretation of Ambiguous Sentences Related to Threat in Anxiety," *Journal of Abnormal Psychology* 100, no. 2 (1991): 144.

2. Aaron T. Beck, *Depression: Clinical, Experimental, and Theoretical Aspects* (New York: Harper Row, 1967).

3. Marsha Linehan, *DBT Skills Training Manual* (Guilford, 2014).

4. Daniel J. Siegel and Tina Payne Bryson, *The Whole-Brain Child: 12 Revolutionary Strategies to Nurture Your Child's Developing Mind* (Random House Digital, 2011).

Chapter 9: Fear, Self-Doubt, Shame, and the Allure of the Comfort Zone

1. Steven C. Hayes, Kirk D. Strosahl, and Kelly G. Wilson, *Acceptance and Commitment Therapy: The Process and Practice of Mindful Change* (Guilford, 2011).

2. Katy Milkman, *How to Change: The Science of Getting from Where You Are to Where You Want to Be* (Penguin, 2021).

3. Daniel Kahneman, *Thinking, Fast and Slow* (Macmillan, 2011).

4. Milkman, *How to Change*.

5. Roy F. Baumeister, "Ego Depletion and Self-Regulation Failure: A Resource Model of Self-Control," *Alcoholism: Clinical and Experimental Research* 27, no. 2 (2003): 281–284.

6. Nir Eyal, *Indistractable: How to Control Your Attention and Choose Your Life* (BenBella Books, 2019).

7. Evan C. Carter, Lilly M. Kofler, Daniel E. Forster, and Michael E. McCullough, "A Series of Meta-Analytic Tests of the Depletion Effect: Self-Control Does Not Seem to Rely on a Limited Resource," *Journal of Experimental Psychology: General* 144, no. 4 (2015): 796.

8. Veronika Job, Carol S. Dweck, and Gregory M. Walton, "Ego Depletion—Is It All in Your Head? Implicit Theories About Willpower Affect Self-Regulation," *Psychological Science* 21, no. 11 (2010): 1686–1693.

Notes

9. *Friends*, season 3, episode 2, "The One Where No One's Ready," directed by Gail Mancuso, aired September 26, 1996, on NBC.
10. Robert Waldinger, "What Makes a Good Life? Lessons from the Longest Study of Happiness," TEDxBeaconStreet video, filmed November 2015 in Brookline, Massachusetts, https://www.ted.com/talks/robert_waldinger_what _makes_a_good_life_lessons_from_the_longest_study_on_happiness.
11. Jason B. Luoma, Barbara S. Kohlenberg, Steven C. Hayes, and Lindsay Fletcher, "Slow and Steady Wins the Race: A Randomized Clinical Trial of Acceptance and Commitment Therapy Targeting Shame in Substance Use Disorders," *Journal of Consulting and Clinical Psychology* 80, no. 1 (2012): 43.
12. Toni Schmader and Brian Lickel, "The Approach and Avoidance Function of Guilt and Shame Emotions: Comparing Reactions to Self-Caused and Other-Caused Wrongdoing," *Motivation and Emotion* 30, no. 1 (2006): 42–55.
13. Brené Brown, *Dare to Lead: Brave Work. Tough Conversations. Whole Hearts* (Random House, 2018).
14. Janina Scarlet, *Unseen, Unheard, and Undervalued: Managing Loneliness, Loss of Connection and Not Fitting In* (Robinson, 2023).
15. Brené Brown, *The Power of Vulnerability: Teachings on Authenticity, Connection, and Courage*, audiobook, read by the author (Sounds True, 2012).

Chapter 11: Getting Comfortable Being Uncomfortable

1. Elisabeth Kübler-Ross and David Kessler, *Life Lessons: Two Experts on Death and Dying Teach Us About the Mysteries of Life and Living* (Simon and Schuster, 2012).
2. Ana I. Masedo and M. Rosa Esteve, "Effects of Suppression, Acceptance and Spontaneous Coping on Pain Tolerance, Pain Intensity and Distress," *Behaviour Research and Therapy* 45, no. 2 (2007): 199–209.
3. Vendela Westin, Richard Östergren, and Gerhard Andersson, "The Effects of Acceptance Versus Thought Suppression for Dealing with the Intrusiveness of Tinnitus," *International Journal of Audiology* 47, no. S2 (2008): S112–S118.
4. Lance M. McCracken, "Learning to Live with the Pain: Acceptance of Pain Predicts Adjustment in Persons with Chronic Pain," *Pain* 74, no. 1 (1998): 21–27.
5. Jill T. Levitt, Timothy A. Brown, Susan M. Orsillo, and David H. Barlow, "The Effects of Acceptance Versus Suppression of Emotion on Subjective and Psychophysiological Response to Carbon Dioxide Challenge in Patients with Panic Disorder," *Behavior Therapy* 35, no. 4 (2004): 747–766.

Chapter 12: Together We Can: Connecting with Community and Changing the World

1. National Center for Education Statistics, *High School and Beyond, 1980: A Longitudinal Survey of Students in the United States* (Inter-university Consortium for Political and Social Research, 2006).

2. Kelly McGonigal, *The Joy of Movement: How Exercise Helps Us Find Happiness, Hope, Connection, and Courage* (Penguin, 2019).

3. Jessica Lahey, *The Addiction Inoculation: Raising Healthy Kids in a Culture of Dependence* (Harper, 2021).

4. Jay J. Van Bavel and Dominic J. Packer, *The Power of Us: Harnessing Our Shared Identities to Improve Performance, Increase Cooperation, and Promote Social Harmony* (Little, Brown Spark, 2021).

5. Ning Xia and Huige Li, "Loneliness, Social Isolation, and Cardiovascular Health," *Antioxidants & Redox Signaling* 28, no. 9 (2018): 837–851.

6. Eve Rodsky, *Find Your Unicorn Space: Reclaim Your Creative Life in a Too-Busy World* (Penguin, 2021).

7. Ed O'Brien and Samantha Kassirer, "People Are Slow to Adapt to the Warm Glow of Giving," *Psychological Science* 30, no. 2 (2019): 193–204.

8. Ericka Sóuter, *How to Have a Kid and a Life: A Survival Guide* (Sounds True, 2021).

9. Geena Davis Institute on Gender in Media (website), https://seejane.org.

10. Callie Womble Edwards, "Overcoming Imposter Syndrome and Stereotype Threat: Reconceptualizing the Definition of a Scholar," *Taboo: The Journal of Culture and Education* 18, no. 1 (2019): 3.

11. Steven J. Spencer, Christine Logel, and Paul G. Davies, "Stereotype Threat," *Annual Review of Psychology* 67, no. 1 (2016): 415–437.

12. Michael Johns, Toni Schmader, and Andy Martens, "Knowing Is Half the Battle: Teaching Stereotype Threat as a Means of Improving Women's Math Performance," *Psychological Science* 16, no. 3 (2005): 175–179.

13. Zoe Chance, *Influence Is Your Superpower: The Science of Willing Hearts, Sparking Change, and Making Good Things Happen* (Random House, 2022).

14. Shiri Cohen, Marc S. Schulz, Emily Weiss, and Robert J. Waldinger, "Eye of the Beholder: The Individual and Dyadic Contributions of Empathic Accuracy and Perceived Empathic Effort to Relationship Satisfaction," *Journal of Family Psychology* 26, no. 2 (2012): 236.

15. Juliana Schroeder, Michael Kardas, and Nicholas Epley, "The Humanizing Voice: Speech Reveals, and Text Conceals, a More Thoughtful Mind in the Midst of Disagreement," *Psychological Science* 28, no. 12 (2017): 1745–1762.

16. Jack Brehm, *A Theory of Psychological Reactance* (Academic Press, 1966).

17. Zoe Chance, "How to Make a Behavior Addictive," TEDxMillRiver video, filmed in 2013, https://www.youtube.com/watch?v=AHfiKav9fcQ.

18. Adam Grant, *Think Again: The Power of Knowing What You Don't Know* (Penguin, 2021).

Chapter 13: Self-Compassion

1. Kristin Neff, *Fierce Self-Compassion: How Women Can Harness Kindness to Speak Up, Claim Their Power, and Thrive* (Penguin UK, 2021).

Notes

2. Paul Gilbert, *Compassion Focused Therapy: Distinctive Features* (Routledge, 2010).
3. Ricks Warren, Elke Smeets, and Kristin Neff, "Self-Criticism and Self-Compassion: Risk and Resilience: Being Compassionate to Oneself Is Associated with Emotional Resilience and Psychological Well-Being," *Current Psychiatry* 15, no. 12 (2016): 18–28.
4. Theodore A. Powers, Richard Koestner, and David C. Zuroff, "Self-Criticism, Goal Motivation, and Goal Progress," *Journal of Social and Clinical Psychology* 26, no. 7 (2007): 826–840.
5. Gilbert, *Compassion Focused Therapy*.
6. Neff, *Fierce Self-Dompassion*.
7. Kristin D. Neff and Roos Vonk, "Self-Compassion Versus Global Self-Esteem: Two Different Ways of Relating to Oneself," *Journal of Personality* 77, no. 1 (2009): 23–50.
8. Filip Raes, "Rumination and Worry as Mediators of the Relationship Between Self-Compassion and Depression and Anxiety," *Personality and Individual Differences* 48, no. 6 (2010): 757–761.
9. Kristin D. Neff, Stephanie S. Rude, and Kristin L. Kirkpatrick, "An Examination of Self-Compassion in Relation to Positive Psychological Functioning and Personality Traits," *Journal of Research in Personality* 41, no. 4 (2007): 908–916.
10. Kristin D. Neff, Kristin L. Kirkpatrick, and Stephanie S. Rude, "Self-Compassion and Its Link to Adaptive Psychological Functioning," *Journal of Research in Personality* 41, no. 1 (2007): 139–154.
11. Kristin D. Neff, "Self-Compassion: An Alternative Conceptualization of a Healthy Attitude Toward Oneself," *Self and Identity* 2, no. 2 (2003): 85–102.
12. Kristin D. Neff, "Self-Compassion: Moving Beyond the Pitfalls of a Separate Self-Concept," in *Transcending Self-Interest: Psychological Explorations of the Quiet Ego*, ed. Jack J. Bauer and Heidi A. Wayment (Washington, DC: APA Books, 2008).
13. Kristin D. Neff, "Self-Compassion, Self-Esteem, and Well-Being," *Social and Personality Psychology Compass* 5, no. 1 (2011): 1–12.
14. Adapted from Jennifer Kemp, *The ACT Workbook for Perfectionism: Build Your Best (Imperfect) Life Using Powerful Acceptance and Commitment Therapy and Self-Compassion Skills* (New Harbinger Publications, 2021).
15. Adapted from Kristin Neff, "Exercise 3: Exploring Self-Compassion Through Writing," Self-Compassion (website), https://self-compassion.org/exercise-3-exploring-self-compassion-writing/.
16. James W. Pennebaker, "Writing About Emotional Experiences as a Therapeutic Process," *Psychological Science* 8, no. 3 (1997): 162–166.
17. Michaela Thomas, *The Lasting Connection: Developing Love and Compassion for Yourself and Your Partner* (Robinson, 2021).
18. Moheb Costandi, *Neuroplasticity* (MIT Press, 2016).
19. James Clear, *Atomic Habits: An Easy & Proven Way to Build Good Habits & Break Bad Ones* (Penguin, 2018).

20. Jason B. Luoma and Melissa G. Platt, "Shame, Self-Criticism, Self-Stigma, and Compassion in Acceptance and Commitment Therapy," *Current Opinion in Psychology* 2 (2015): 97–101.
21. Kevin E. Vowles, Katie Witkiewitz, Gail Sowden, and Julie Ashworth, "Acceptance and Commitment Therapy for Chronic Pain: Evidence of Mediation and Clinically Significant Change Following an Abbreviated Interdisciplinary Program of Rehabilitation," *Journal of Pain* 15, no. 1 (2014): 101–113.

Chapter 14: Keep Going

1. Elisabeth Kübler-Ross and David Kessler, *Life Lessons: Two Experts on Death and Dying Teach Us About the Mysteries of Life and Living* (Simon and Schuster, 2012).

Index

Index

Index

About the Author

JILL STODDARD is passionate about sharing science-backed ideas from psychology to help people thrive. She is a psychologist, TEDx speaker, award-winning teacher, peer-reviewed ACT trainer, and cohost of the popular *Psychologists Off the Clock* podcast. Dr. Stoddard is the author of two other books: *Be Mighty: A Woman's Guide to Liberation from Anxiety, Worry, and Stress Using Mindfulness and Acceptance* and *The Big Book of ACT Metaphors: A Practitioner's Guide to Experiential Exercises and Metaphors in Acceptance and Commitment Therapy*. Her writing has also appeared in *Psychology Today,* Scary Mommy, Thrive Global, the Good Men Project, and Mindful Return. She regularly appears on podcasts and as an expert source for various media outlets. She lives in Newburyport, Massachusetts, with her husband, two kids, and disobedient French bulldog.